First We Have Coffee

by

Margaret T. Jensen

THOMAS NELSON PUBLISHERS

NASHVILLE

Published in Nashville, Tennessee, by Thomas Nelson, Inc.

Scripture references are from the King James Version of the
Bible.

Library of Congress Cataloging-in-Publication Data

Jensen, Margaret T. (Margaret Twenten), 1916–
    First we have coffee / by Margaret T. Jensen.
        p.   cm.
    Originally published: San Bernardino, Calif. : Here's
Life Publishers, 1982.
    ISBN 0-8407-4284-3 (pbk.)
    1. Tweten, Elius N., d. 1973. 2. Tweten, Ella. d. 1977.
3. Baptists — Clergy — Biography. 4. Clergymen's
wives — Biography. I. Title.
[BX6493.JK46   1993]
286 .0922 – dc20
[B]   92-45197
                                                            CIP

Printed in the United States of America

16 17 18 19 20 — 97 96 95 94 93

Dedicated to
Mama's other children

Bernice, Grace, Gordon Lund, Doris,
Joyce Solveig, Jeanelle.

Although separated from some by miles and from others
by death, we remain united by the divine cord of love. We
were born sisters and brother, but we chose each other for
friends. I thank God for memories shared with them.

Contents

A SPECIAL THANK YOU

To my husband, Harold, who had to have the gift of interpretation to be able to transfer my penned scrawl to the typewriter. The trial of that kind of faith brought forth patience — enough to keep encouraging me daily. He just kept supplying me with more pens and yellow pads of paper. He thought I was the greatest storyteller, and because I believed him, I kept on writing.

To our precious daughter, Janice Jensen Carlberg, who continues to be a source of joy and encouragement to her family. Besides being a beautiful wife and mother, she is also a gifted writer, sending her words, alive with faith, across the miles to bring light into dark places, and trust where doubt lingers. Jan constantly encouraged me to be myself and tell my stories my own way. I DID!

To Christine Fisher Jensen, God's special gift of love to our youngest son, Ralph. She is not only the sister Jan longed for, but a special gift of joy to all the family. Chris would stop in the middle of dishes or diapers to be a sounding board for her mom's endless stories.

To Dale Hanson Bourke and to Kelsey Menehen, from *Today's Christian Woman*, who had the courage to publish my short stories and keep me writing more. Thank you for permission to use excerpts from the stories "High Button Shoes," "Bowl of Cherries" and "The Dress."

To Dr. Gordon Macdonald, pastor of Grace Chapel, Lexington, Massachusetts, for his encouragement and suggested title, "First We Have Coffee."

To Dr. R. Judson Carlberg (my son-in-law), Dean of the faculty of Gordon College, Wenham, Massachusetts, who encouraged me to attend my first writer's conference at Gordon College. Perhaps he was hoping I would write my stories so he wouldn't have to listen to them over and over again.

To Leslie H. Stobbe, Editorial Director, Here's Life Publishers, Inc., who walked by faith and not by sight, and dared to tunnel through words to make a dream possible.

To Evelyn Bence, author, editor, poet, my teacher, who had the courage to delete and the wisdom to add a period.

Introduction

Sunday, January 16, 1977, 2:00 P.M. Bracing against the wind, the young and old quietly entered the First Baptist Church of Stoneville, North Carolina. Five sisters and their families sat in a front row. I, Margaret, the eldest, felt comfort in the presence of Mama's other living daughters: Grace, Doris, Joyce, and the "baby," Jeanelle.

The quiet service defied the blizzard raging on the other side of the church walls. The Reverend Mr. J. Ward Burch assured us of God's presence. "Let not your heart be troubled," he read, then continued with old familiar hymns and other favorite Scripture passages.

A settled faith lingered in our hearts as we silently followed the gray casket into the icy wind. "I'm glad Mama is warm," I thought, "and can't feel this wind, so reminiscent of the Saskatchewan winters."

Within a few minutes the cars slid slowly over the frozen road toward the family cemetery, to the graveside where the canopy whipped in the wind. I found myself remembering Canada and Mama's long hand-knit ski pants carefully tucked under her flowing dress. I thought I felt her hand as I trudged across the snow to her final place of rest. Had the Canadian wind come to North Carolina to say farewell?

The small cemetery held two older graves covered with snow. Huddled in coats and scarves, we braced each other around the open grave, and remembered our two loved ones whom Mother was joining — our father and their only son, Gordon.

Nearby, the big house, home of my sister Doris and her husband David Hammer, stood like a sentinel against the sky. Its chimney sent smoke signals to the snow-covered wooded hills. Across the road Mama's yellow house slept empty and silent, the coffee pot cold.

The defiant wind could not sweep away the majestic words — they returned again and again, echoing through the valley. "LORD, Thou hast been our dwelling place in all generations. Surely goodness and mercy shall follow me all the days of my life: and I will dwell in the house of the LORD for ever."

Slowly we walked to the big house where logs blazed and coffee perked. As old stories and familiar hymns filled the air, the warmth of friendship and loving memories filled our hearts.

With coffee cup in hand I moved close to the fire to watch the flaming logs. An amber glow of love and warmth engulfed me and I knew that Mama lived on somewhere beyond the storm, safely in the house of the Lord for ever.

I also knew that I had to write the story of Mama and her Norwegian coffee, poured with that same amber glow of love.

Being the eldest, I remembered much. The story began for me when I found Mama's Norwegian diary in the right hand corner of an old chest — but before we start, first we have coffee.

one

The Diary

IT SEEMS LIKE YESTERDAY; I held the black book in my hand and whispered to my sister Grace, "Close the door."

In front of me sat an enraptured audience of sisters and girl friends. All promised never to tell and I unfolded the script of a secret drama. In the 1930s we created our own theatrical productions.

Out of Mama's diary, carefully hidden in the right hand corner of an old chest, I rendered a not-too-literal translation from Norwegian to English, and wove a story of romance and intrigue. This production should have received a Tony Award.

From the pages of the black book emerged my mother, Elvine Johannessen, as a fifteen-year-old girl, standing on the deck of the majestic ocean liner, The United States.

Her tears said goodbye to Norway's town of Lista, and, in the back fields of her mind, she planted happy memories of the midnight sun, fjords, and fishing boats; perhaps the ocean would roll away the painful memories of childhood. Like waves that beat against a ship; bitterness pounded against Elvine. As long as the waves stayed on the outside there was no danger, but bitterness, like waves, brought destruction when allowed to penetrate walls.

She set her sights on the future; in America she would see her beautiful, mysterious mother, and her beloved brother, Joe, who had preceded her across the ocean.

As the sun swept across the water and the moon made a silvery highway over the waves, there was time to think. Someday she would learn why her mother had fled to America and left Joe and her when she was only five years old. Deep in Elvine's heart lay the poignant memory of crying out, "Mor, Mor (Mother, Mother)." But her cries had gone unheeded. Her sobbing mother had continued walking away from her, never to return, and her austere aunt had severely scolded, "Do not call her Mor, call her Tilda."

With a toss of her head, Elvine had defiantly declared her ownership, "Min mor (My mother)."

With trembling hands Elvine clutched her knit shawl around her shoulders and followed her fellow immigrants onto the deck. The majestic ocean liner was easing into the mouth of the New York harbor. Ahead of her stood the lovely lady, the Statue of Liberty. Ahead of her lay the land of hope and glory.

The next day Elvine felt small and alone in the notorious clamor of Ellis Island's endless inspections and army of officials. But it was all erased from her mind when she saw her beautiful, rebellious mother who had defied tradition and sailed to America. Someday she would learn the rest of the story. Today it was enough to hear, "Min kjare Elvine (My dear Elvine)."

Elvine began her new life in America as a servant girl in a lovely Jewish home on Park Avenue, New York City. While working there she changed her name to Ella. From her wise mistress she learned to love the world of books, music, and poetry. She worked with her hands as she learned with her heart.

Dressed in a deep-blue dress, Bible in hand, Miss Ella walked to the Baptist Mission to hear the new pastor, The Reverend Mr. Elius N. Tweten. "What blue eyes," she thought. His blond hair swept back from a handsome high forehead. As the young Norwegian pastor, himself an orphan, and in America just a few years, looked over this, his first congregation, his gaze, falling on Miss Ella, met the most beautiful eyes he had ever seen. In that moment he determined, "She will be my wife."

What began with conversation over a cup of hot chocolate after church, blossomed into marriage, just three months later.

"Margaret, I didn't know you read Norwegian so well. It's time you started attending the Norwegian services as well as the English."

Mama stood in the doorway, determined to end our fun. She took the book from me and, with misty eyes, softly added, "Someday, I will tell the rest."

I never saw the diary again.

two

The Call

"SIR." THE LIBRARIAN STOOD OVER PAPA'S SHOULDER, interrupting his reading. "It is closing time. You'll have to leave now."

"Oh!" Papa looked up, not wanting to believe the librarian. As usual, time had gotten away from him, but today, he knew, it shouldn't have. "I got married yesterday, and I forgot . . ."

Papa caught the last subway to Brooklyn. When he walked through the door of their honeymoon flat, Mama was reminded of the advice her mother had given her earlier in the day: "Take him as he is and you will be happy. He loves God, the library – and you – in that order. Always keep dinner warm in the oven."

Keep dinner warm, she did.

She loved him, this boy preacher from Norway who had been sent by the ministers of Oslo to study at Morgan Park Seminary in Chicago. He had been hard-working – tending furnaces and waiting on tables to help pay for his tuition, his beloved books, his degree.

I don't know if Mama, on her wedding day, had any idea what "the call" meant. It was more than a call to preach the gospel and serve God's people. It involved a call to pack and move to new community after new community. It involved leaving the familiar and seeking new ground that needed planting. It meant following her charming minister husband, who was *so* spiritually minded, but not at all encumbered with working out the practical details of life. It wasn't long before Papa felt the tug of "the call." God's work in Wisconsin needed Elius Tweten.

The train pulled into the station at Woodville, Wisconsin. Mama, dressed in her wide hat, long coat, and high button shoes caught a glimpse of her new surroundings. Papa's call was to preach. Her call was to make her family a home in this wilderness. The battle for survival had made the welcoming congregation of immigrants strong like oaks, trees of righteousness withstanding the storms of spring and blizzards of winter. They had weathered hardships of such magnitude that they didn't notice the hidden needs of a lonely young wife who had come to learn her husband lived in another world — of his call, his Bible, his libraries, and his favorite second-hand bookstores. His scholarly mind thirsted for books like a desert thirsts for water. Taking Mama by the hand, walking and talking to her about the beauty around them never occurred to him. He silently loved Mama. She understood.

She propped poems on the window sills and pinned them to curtains. She filled her heart with music and poetry. As her hands worked endlessly to sew, scrub, bake, and touch the sick and lonely, she blended love and compassion with Papa's theology.

It was here I was born, Margaret Louise, on Bestemor (Grandmother) Bertilda's birthday, April 18, 1916. Mama poured all the love she had missed into me by singing me songs and telling me endless stories. She sang the Norwegian "So Ro Til Fiske Shar" right alongside the American "Rock-bye Baby." We rode the country lanes together; strapped to her waist, I held her close as she sat upright in the buggy and snapped the reins of the horse.

Papa, a circuit-rider, preached to the forest and hills as he traveled among his scattered, hardy congregation for several years until "the call" came again.

"The call" brought us back to Brooklyn. (Bestemor must have sent an S.O.S. to heaven.)

December bustled with the usual preparations for Christmas, but with a few unusual complications. Mother was expecting the arrival of a new baby, and I had just recovered from diphtheria and returned home from the hospital's contagious ward. Golden-haired Bernice, two years of age, slipped into Papa's study and made uneven rows of his priceless books, then she quietly crawled up into Papa's lap and begged to be rocked to the accompaniment of a Norwegian lullaby. Munching on a piece of Bestemor's delicious yule cake she mumbled her approval, "Godt godt (Good, good)."

But in a few days Papa returned to the dreaded contagious ward with a bundle clutched in his arms. Bernice had contracted diphtheria.

Poor Mama. That night, December 23, 1919, Grace was born and nine days later the winds from the cold Atlantic mourned across the snow-covered graveyard where three lonely figures stood beside a tiny coffin. Mama was home nurturing new life, while Papa, Pastor Otto Hansen, and Mama's brother, Joe, escorted Bernice to her rest.

Shivering in the cold, Pastor Hansen read John 14:1: "Let not your heart be troubled."

Joe stood beside Papa, quietly grieving. Papa seemed to relive hearing Mama's final instructions, given through a dry sob: "Put the woolen socks on Bernice, and don't forget her blanket." Then she had turned to the wall and wept alone, baby Grace sleeping beside her.

Pastor Hansen continued, "In my Father's house are many mansions."

"Ya, that is true," thought Papa. "I must preach more on heaven. Earth holds such sorrow." He seemed to feel the soft, golden hair on his cheeks as he had rocked her. The socks? Ya, he had remembered the woolen socks and the blanket, for Mama's sake.

Joe's arm reached around Papa's shoulder, "Come, it is time to go."

Oh no, he couldn't go and leave Bernice alone in the wind. He had to rock her in the warm blanket.

Pastor Hansen's voice overwhelmed Papa's thoughts: " 'I am the resurrection and the life.' She is alive forevermore." He had heard the same words at another graveside many years ago. The pain of loss was the same and it never went away: the loneliness of a nine-year-old boy calling across the valley for his mother who had left his world to join another.

"Come," repeated Uncle Joe. "We must go home now. Mama is waiting. Bernice is with Jesus."

Like silent shadows the three walked across the frozen ground as falling snow blanketed the tiny grave.

The small flat was warm with light. Bestemor had coffee ready. Mama nursed baby Grace. I helped Bestemor by putting sugar lumps on the table. Papa went to his books and wept softly when he viewed the uneven rows.

Mama's young face had quiet peace, for she had dealt with her grief at the throne of grace. God's promises would never fail! She had looked unto the hills and found, in God, a very present help in her time of trouble.

Some travel the high road in the hills, from peak to peak, where light lingers longer. Some travel in the valleys where they walk in the darkness of their own shadow. Mama would choose to walk the high road with God. She would walk in the light of His grace.

Taking Bestemor's hand, I pointed to the sky and gave my own grief to God. "God made an exchange. He took Bernice and gave us Grace." Bernice, too, had had a "call."

three

Norwegian Holidays in Canada

AT THE NEW YORK CITY STATION we said good-by to Bestemor and boarded a train — to answer "the call" to the First Norwegian Baptist Church in Winnipeg, Manitoba.

At the far end of our trip Mr. Meyer, of the Ellen Street Hotel, met us with a hearty "Velkommen, velkommen (Welcome, welcome)" and swooped me up into his big arms with a Norwegian kiss. His mustache, wet with coffee, brushed my face. His warm welcome was a foretaste of things to come. Every Sunday morning I braced myself for the damp, coffee kiss.

The gray parsonage loomed like a castle against the blue Canadian sky. After getting my bearings inside the house, I set out to explore the larger new world. By the end of the day I sat in the lost-and-found department of the Winnipeg police station.

While the policeman's wife fried fish in a black skillet, her husband soaked his feet in a tub of hot water. It had been a long day for all of us. Happily, I crawled up in his lap to answer his probing questions.

"Today is my birthday," I proudly announced, "and I'm five years old. No, my daddy doesn't work, he just reads books. Mama sings and tells stories. I live in a big castle. Mr. Meyer has a coffee kiss. Bestemor lives in Brooklyn, New York. I came on a train. Papa had a call. Don't you have a little girl? I'm hungry."

The policeman seemed to choke on his words as he told me that his five-year-old daughter had died. By the time the fish dinner was ready, I had helped the policeman dry his feet and put on soft woolen socks and slippers. At the table I promptly asked a Norwegian blessing and launched into Papa's theology. "Your little girl is not dead. She is at home in heaven with Bernice. God is taking care of her until you come. Papa says we have to be ready. The greatest verse in the Bible is John 3:16: 'For God so loved the world, that He gave his only begotten Son, that whosoever believeth in Him should not perish, but have everlasting life.' I'll sing a Norwegian song for you, 'Himmel og jord kan brenner.' Mama sings it all the time and it means that everything can pass away, but God never fails."

Mama had taught me well, but she had never served me a fish dinner like this one.

Suddenly, "Vell, vell," boomed the voice of Mr. Meyer. "Here ve have the little vun."

There, in the doorway, stood Papa — and another coffee kiss.

Reluctantly I kissed my new friends good-by and left with a polite "Thank you for my birthday party." I did not want to disgrace Papa's ministry.

Lured by the lumber companies' recruiting programs, Scandinavian youth headed to the big woods in search of wealth and adventure. Room and board, pay after six months work — it sounded like the pot of gold at the end of a rainbow. But many staggered back, unable to endure the rigors of the demanding life and the intolerable housing conditions. In bitter despair, with no pay, many knocked at the door of the parsonage on Ellen Street.

Mama took them in. She was always ready to sleep another heartbroken wayfarer.

A Jewish salesman saved his woolen samples of cloth for Mama's quilts, which became pallets spread across the floor on which we children slept. Mama filled the beds with homeless immigrants and missionaries. I was convinced that heaven was a place where we would have our own beds.

For a Norwegian, all hardships are forgotten on two days a year: the seventeenth of May, Norway's Independence Day, and Christmas Eve.

Every seventeenth of May, we marched in Norwegian national dress: red, white, and blue embroidered caps and dresses. The boys wore dark trousers and embroidered shirts and caps. Bands played. Free concerts in the park were followed by Norwegian statesmen pouring forth golden oratory about the glories of the old country, always adding a stern admonition to bring honor to the new land.

Everyone shared the hardships, and thus the

burdens dwindled. Everyone shared the triumphs, and thus the joys multiplied. Singing the Norwegian national anthem, "Ja vi elsker dette landet (Yes, we love this land)" filled the crowd with memories of the Land of the Midnight Sun and caused them to dedicate themselves afresh to honorable service in the new land. At the end of the festivities the immigrants returned to their labors with renewed hope for another year.

And Christmas Eve. It also brought life to the driest bones. One such night I will never forget.

On the corner, next to the parsonage, stood the old church. Her spire touched the stars. The warm lights that streamed from the many windows sprinkled the snow with millions of diamonds. The relentless winds of a Canadian winter (just forty degrees below zero) whipped fantastic patterns on the frost-covered windows. Inside the creaking walls, a large parlor floor supported a huge spruce tree. The star on the top touched the ceiling and every imaginable homemade decoration trimmed the boughs. Small candles in make-shift candle holders were placed evenly around the huge tree which stood in the center of the room. Tonight was the greatest night of all the year.

My sister Grace, brother Gordon, and new baby sister, Doris, and I had been scrubbed shiny pink and poured into new white, long flannel underwear, an annual gift. The scrubbings were a weekly event. We had that down pat. Papa scrubbed. Mama dried. I, the big sister "poured."

This afternoon we were all promptly put to bed for an afternoon nap. How could anyone nap with so much excitement in the air? But nap, we did, with persuasion. Papa, the persuader, stood by the door.

How could anyone explain the complete joy and expectancy when our naps were over and the thrill of getting dressed for this night of nights filled our young hearts. Mama had, of course, made all the long underwear. We topped that with starched petticoats and ruffled bloomers. Then finally, we donned her masterpiece, our Christmas dresses. The long white stockings, properly fastened with store-bought garters, and the big, colorful, stiff hairbows which matched the dresses provided the perfect finishing touches.

Mama, the angel of Christmas, had treadled the old machine through the quiet night hours to prepare our clothes and small gifts. Papa had helped out by walking with the croupy little ones, preaching endless sermons into their ears.

But tonight their work was over. We all were well and every need had been miraculously supplied through another year. Mama had prepared large platters of lutefisk, part of the traditional Norwegian Christmas dinner. We children begged for meatballs instead of the special fish, but one scornful glance from Mama and we ate lutefisk, a slippery, tasteless fish). Beautiful casseroles of rice pudding baked in the oven of the old cookstove. Dozens of loaves of Mama's bread and Jule Kakke (Yule cake) cooled on the kitchen table. Vegetables and fruits added color to the festivities, as did the decorated cookies.

"Here they come," Papa shouted as he heard the steps crunching in the snow. Very dignified in his black suit and starched collar, he stood at the door and welcomed the guests. Who were they?

No, not relatives coming home for Christmas. Having followed "the call," we were far away from loved ones, in a lonely land of strangers. These guests were the lonely Scandinavian immigrants who sat at the railroad station on Christmas Eve day. They were the forgotten ones who congregated at the station, keeping one another company while watching for incoming trains.

That day, as was his routine, Papa visited the railroad station to offer his assistance to the strangers. When he realized that these men (about fifteen of them) had no place to go, he gave an open invitation to come to the parsonage for the traditional Christmas Eve celebration.

They were disillusioned strangers — hungry — and so alone. Filled with dreams, they had come to a land of promise and they were ashamed to return home without their pot of gold. Sweethearts, wives, and mothers waited for them in the faraway Land of the Midnight Sun.

But tonight, this night of nights, the look of despair changed to hope with Papa's hearty "Velkommen, velkommen (Welcome, welcome)."

Snow-flaked fur caps, coats and overshoes were placed near the stove to dry. The musical instruments brought by the guests (at Papa's request) were opened to tune up for the impromptu concert after dinner.

My memory of the immigrants is that they were blonde, rosy-cheeked, blue-eyed, and wore navy-blue serge suits. Under their arms they usually had a guitar, mandolin or flute. That Christmas was no exception.

Mama, as always, was prepared for the unexpected, and with her compassionate heart made each stranger feel a part of the family. "Ven you have heart room you have house room," she reminded us often.

Just as the guests were seated around the table there was the sound of stomping feet on the porch. From out of the cold emerged two half-frozen men, Barney and John, who had fled the big woods. They had defied the Canadian winter and made it back to Winnipeg for Christmas Eve. Trekking over eighty miles of ice and snow, they were sustained by a burning desire to reach the only home they knew in the new land for Christmas Eve. Rescue stations along the way had served hot tea and biscuits to the desperate travelers. But now they were home, and it was Christmas.

Around that evening's festive table old hurts were forgotten and hope, faith and courage for tomorrow were rekindled.

Mama always looked like an angel with shining eyes — even if she didn't have a new dress for Christmas. "I'll get one later," she whispered to me. Barney recounted his adventures with a flourish, while John basked in the warmth of the fireside and food. The other guests now were no longer strangers — we all seemed like one big family.

As Papa read the Christmas story, we envisioned angels and shepherds and the dear little Babe in the manger. Strange how little we knew of holiday rush, Santa Claus, and expensive gifts. After dinner we gathered in the parlor to join hands, march around the Christmas tree and sing old Norwegian songs and carols. We opened the gifts. No one had been left out. We welcomed handkerchiefs, aprons, new hairbows, apples, one orange each, and some candy. Any small toy was a rare delight beyond words. Mama made sure that each guest received a small gift.

While the men tuned their instruments, Papa struck the chords of the piano with a flourish. Violins, mandolins, and guitars blended with the piano against the lonely sound of a plaintive flute. Voices raised in joyful song, blended in harmony like a great choir. Standing tall and straight I sang with them in the grand finale — "Den Himmelske Lovsang (The Heavenly Song of Praise)." I can still remember that sound. I was nine years old. Papa closed in prayer. He lifted up to the throne of God each one of us in the room, and then he left each of us safe and secure in His keeping. Christmas Eve was the night of nights, the prelude to tomorrow, Christmas Day, when church bells would ring out across the sparkling snow, calling the people to worship. Mama would sit straight with her little ones in a row. Papa, in his Prince Albert coat, would announce the opening hymn.

> Joy to the world; the Lord has come.
> Let earth receive her King.

four

The Touch

As the immigration trains continued to chug into Winnipeg, Papa continued to bring the homeless to Mother. Papa untangled the web of humanity that came his way by telling them of his undying faith in God and in Mama. Mama wove for them a web of pure gold, the gold of love.

During this time a woman with six children became a part of our family while her husband worked in the big woods.

That same winter the whooping cough struck in force. We each whooped into his or her own tin. I remember finding a warm spot behind the kitchen stove, and there whooping until thoroughly exhausted. I fell asleep with my head in the wood box.

At night Papa walked the floor until a blond head slept on his shoulder.

Our immediate family fared well, but not all our congregation was as strong or full of vigor.

On one of her errands of mercy, Mama heard the cries of a young woman. Climbing the stairs to the attic flat, Mother heard, "Oh, God! Help me, please help me." Inside she found a terrified, expectant young mother whose husband also was working in the big woods.

That night we set up a bed in the parlor. A little later a baby was born. When the husband returned from the woods he found a tiny casket, surrounded by men in navy-blue serge suits, in the parlor. Papa, conducting his first funeral in Winnipeg comforted the grief-stricken woodsman with the words of John 14:1: "Let not your heart be troubled." Papa knew the man's heart, as Papa remembered Bernice and the mourning coastal wind. Mama's love enfolded the young mother, for she, too, remembered Bernice.

Very shortly, the dark clouds of another impending storm broke and a flu epidemic engulfed the immigrants. Mama went from one house to the other, caring for the sick and dying. Her own house also needed her. She arose to tend a crying child and the ailing furnace. There was no use in calling Papa; he was critically ill. She would have to do the fixing herself. Walking toward the cellar stairs, she crumpled, her own strength suddenly drained from her. To us, Mama (in her early thirties, slender and beautiful) was ageless, the symbol of life itself, the Statue of Liberty built on the Rock of Ages. This night she wept alone.

"Oh God," she cried. "One day in bed, is that so much to ask? Oh God, strength to tend this furnace, is that so much to ask?"

Softly as a whisper in the night, a Presence drew near. "Why don't you ask Me to heal you? There is nothing too hard for Me."

"Oh yes, Jesus. Heal me, and I will use my strength to serve You."

"Inasmuch as ye have done it unto one of the least of these My brethren, ye have done it unto Me," Matthew 25:40, ran through her mind. Warmth and light engulfed her as she felt the power of God's healing love surge through her weary body.

She arose and thanked God; she tended the children and stoked the furnace. Her refreshing sleep was sweet.

God had touched His precious child with the amber glow of His divine love; she in turn, gave it away — to His children.

One of the Christmas wayfarers received that touch of divine love through Mama and became a permanent family member. When Barney had first stumbled into the parlor, he had handed Mama his whiskey bottle, then knelt in repentance while Papa prayed for his soul. Mama never told us what she did with the whiskey the parlor converts gave her.

Barney became our link to the outside world, where people were brave and cowardly, strong and weak, loving and hateful, great and small, noble and mean. Barney brought us reality and humor.

While the coffee pot perked on the stove and Mama kneaded dough for tomorrow's bread, Barney strummed his mandolin and sang the folk songs of Norway. Barney had the power to persuade Papa to leave his books and dance a polka as we clapped in rhythm. The agony and ecstasy of life was always with us; we learned to capitalize on the joy of any moment.

Barney told stories of his life as a newspaper man

in Oslo. As a boxer he had been wild and rebellious, but finally tamed by a beautiful golden-haired blue-eyed fisherman's daughter. One day she had gone to sea with her father. The fishing boat had never returned. He had searched the seashore and called to the waves, but only silence had greeted him.

In desperation he had come to America — to forget. "Out of all things, God works together for good," Mama repeatedly reminded him as she baked her bread or cooked her famous vegetable soup.

There was always a wildness about him as he winked his brown eyes at all the pretty girls. "Bjarne (Barney), you must get a good wife and settle down," Mama would often say.

"How can I help it if God gave me such a big heart with room to love them all?"

When he saw an injustice he exploded, "Lucky for you I'm not God!" As we grew older he followed "Mama's girls" around at church picnics in case the boys had a few ideas of their own. When there was no money for an ice cream cone, Barney managed to dole out a few nickels. Years later when we fell in love, he listened. When Papa's unreasonable demands made life difficult, Barney talked to Papa. His mandolin played "Just Molly and Me," or "I'm Coming Back to You," and the girls fell in love with him and his music.

Heeding Mama's admonition to "settle down with a good wife," Barney finally married a comfortable friend, Mildred, who was solid, faithful and strong and became his harbor in the storms of life.

Within him still pounded the restless waves that batter Norway's rocky coast, the waves that had buried his love. Walking the New York City seacoast, or the trails of Central Park, he was an easy victim to passions hidden within. A fleeting escape from his harbor once brought him crashing to shore like human driftwood. Like King David of old he cried out in anguish "I have sinned against heaven and earth. Cleanse me, oh God!" Black despair engulfed him until he found himself on the Brooklyn Bridge — looking for an escape.

Unnoticed in the shadows a silent figure, who had stood quietly waiting, saw the stooped figure of despair. Suddenly Barney felt an arm around his shoulders, "Let's go home to Mama for a cup of coffee." In silence Papa took Barney home to Mama.

Later Barney found his harbor, Mildred, waiting and forgiving. The storm had passed. Barney was safe in the arms of the Lord who said, "I love you with an everlasting love." Together Mildred and Barney served the Lord for many years and became a harbor for others.

The Children's Uncle Barney

Some leave monuments of fame,
A sweeping sunset done in oil,
A bridge to span the ocean wave,
An empire built from common toil.

But down life's road there comes but one
Who spins his magic on a child,
That bit of gold when day is done,
Weaver of stories, sweet and wild.

His wide brown eyes of mystery,
Enchanting smile that children know,
He drew them close upon his knee
And sang sweet songs of long ago.

This one — a part of life and daring
Who loved, not wisely, but too well —
Came from the cliffs and fjords, bearing
Tales from craggy coast and snowy dell.

With battered mandolin and plaintive tune,
He sang of lovers lost at sea —
Golden hair, a windswept dune,
The ocean crossing over the lee.

With him we climbed the rugged cliffs
Or sailed the seas across the foam
And fought great storms in iron ships,
But never failed to come back home.

And always there would be tomorrow
Dime store trips — a lollipop,
An ice cream cone for childish sorrow,
A splash of sun on a small rain drop.

This world of dreams and make believe
Belongs to children, full of wonder.
The years find time enough to grieve;
Let childhood keep the right to ponder.

Hand in hand, he walked with us;
Bending low, he wiped a tear.
Side by side he talked with us
And listened to each childish fear.

"Some day they'll say old Barney's gone.
Don't you believe it — no grief for me.
I'll be singing a glory song
With heaven's children round my knee."

Some build monuments of fame,
A life of victory and power.
But one walked gently childhood's lane
And left us with one shining hour.

five

All Through the Week

MAMA AND PAPA, LIKE GOD, never slumbered nor slept. What a comfort — waking in the night to the sound of the treadle sewing machine and Papa preaching sermons to the dark or practicing his English. How he wanted to remove the Scandinavian accent from his speech. He would shout, "I got it, I got it, Mama. I don't say 'ven' anymore, I say 'ven!' Mama, we must speak good English ven we are in America."

Monday mornings, Papa emerged, in white shirt and tie, to take his place by the washing machine. He held a book in one hand and powered the agitator with the other. While Mama sliced Naptha soap into the hot water, she sang "What can wash away my sin?" Paying her no mind, Papa continued reading aloud, practicing English diction.

One look at the clothesline told the neighbors how often we changed underwear or how many overnight guests Mama had taken in. In the winter the frozen long underwear looked like ghosts hovering in the sky.

Not only was Monday washday, it was also soup day. The scraps dropped into the kettle of homemade soup and the loaves of Mama's rye bread seemed to multiply like the loaves and fishes in the New Testament story. Regardless of the number of unexpected guests, there was always enough. God and Mama could do anything!

Tuesday was ironing day. A basket of clothes which had been sprinkled and rolled and left to stand overnight was now ready for the all-day ordeal. As the irons heated on the stove, Mama washed the dishes and made the beds. Every sheet was ironed. When Mama finished with them, the ruffles on starched petticoats, dresses, and aprons stood out like rows of fences. As Mama ironed, she taught. Her methods were simple: endless songs and stories and Bible verses for us to memorize. I sat enthralled, listening, watching, and waiting for the day I could iron the dishtowels, then the starched pillowcases, and then graduate to Papa's white handkerchiefs, which had to be perfectly folded. No one but Mama ever ironed Papa's white Sunday shirt or the treasured Sunday-dinner linen tablecloth!

At noon, Mama always stopped for lunch and naptime. No one — on any day — escaped the nap. Papa went quietly to his study. The house grew still. The children slept. Mama rested thirty minutes (surely she didn't sleep), then rose quietly. She brushed out her long brown hair and put on a crisp starched dress and apron. To complete her preparations for the second half of her day, she sat down and opened her Bible. After reading, she quietly slipped to her knees for her afternoon talk with God. Mama's prayer time was as sure as the sun coming up in the morning. Even the youngest child knew to be quiet until Mama finished.

The Bible closed, Mama, smelling fresh like Palmolive soap and starch, put on the coffee pot. That was the sign that made the sleepy house bound with life. Papa emerged from the study. The children, dressed in starched, afternoon clothing, came to the table for "coffee." For the children, hot water with milk and sugar accompanied the rye bread and jam and the coveted treat — a lump of sugar dipped in Papa's coffee. Papa then left to visit the widows and orphans, but not without a word of caution from Mama about the widows.

Ironing days were full of talk. Childish problems and questions were discussed in this classroom disguised as Mama's kitchen. Papa was unreachable. Within him spanned the stretch of the mountains, the depth of the valley, the pounding of the surf, and the lonely cry of the sea gull. He could place a compassionate arm around a man stumbling in the gutter and lead him to God, but he couldn't hear his children say, "Talk to us, Father!" He couldn't reach us, but he gave us the best that he had — Mama. To him she was a ruby without price, the woman above all women who would show his children how to obey his commands and daily live out the "why" of them. Slowly, but well, we learned — by word, by example, and sometimes "by strap."

In the pantry corner hung a red strap, which held a high place of dignity and honor in the eyes of us four children. One parental glance in that general direction was usually enough to call the troops to attention. No other humiliation could match that of the bending, drawers down, and bare "rumpa" exposed to the world, over Mama's knee. The pain inflicted by the strap was minimal in comparison to the shame of the hanging drawers and the knowledge that you had somehow "disgraced the ministry."

"Children obey your parents," was one of the first Bible verses I ever learned.

One day in a moment of anger, I stuck out my tongue at our neighbor (albeit behind his back). Not only did I encounter the strap, but red pepper on my tongue. And I suffered through a face-to-face apology. The verse for the day was, "Be ye kind one to another." Discipline was swift and sure! In fact it was so sure that often we reached for the strap and red pepper and pulled down our drawers — the sooner done, the better. There was no escape. Just as sure as the punishment, however, was the sense of cleansing and forgiveness. Our slate was clean. The touch of love was a soft, warm glow.

Wednesday was mending day. Mama slipped the wooden egg into the stockings and her fingers flew, in and out, until a hole was no more. I sat beside her busy at work with a piece of cloth, a needle, and a thread. Patiently she loosened my endless knots, and we started again, until I eventually learned her tricks.

Thursday was visiting day. Hand in hand, we took homemade bread and jars of soup to the lonely and sick. In the afternoon a clean, starched tablecloth covered the table, and china cups were set for afternoon coffee. As we had visited others, so guests were sure to visit us.

Friday was baking day. The dough had been kneaded the night before — to the music of our friend Barney's mandolin. Papa sometimes turned the heavy dough until it was ready for rising. Thursday nights we fell asleep to the smell of yeast and the sound of the mandolin. Friday's reward was the end crust, covered with melted butter. By late Friday afternoon, Mama would have a warm line-up of ten loaves of bread, a sponge cake for Sunday dinner and, we hoped, some soft cookies plump with raisins.

Saturday — cleaning day. In case there was a shortage of godliness, Mama made up for it with cleanliness. By the time I was seven, she had taught me to do the dishes (properly): wash, rinse, dry, put away, scour the sink, sweep the floor, and put out the garbage. No one, but *no one*, ever left unwashed dishes in the sink. That would be a blot on the ministry that not even God could overlook. When I visited in other homes and saw unwashed dishes, I promptly pulled up a chair to the sink and started washing. I wouldn't allow anyone else to disgrace their ministry, either.

Discipline and order went together, just as coffee and sugar lumps went together.

Our wall motto about the unseen guest in our home, the listener to every conversation, was a reality. God lived in our house. It had to be clean in every way.

Saturday morning involved a literal "rise and shine." Every child had a task. The stove was polished a shiny black. Every chair was scrubbed or polished. Every floor — nook and cranny — felt the power of Fels Naptha soap and a scrub brush. No dallying, every task was accomplished by nap time, or else!

Afternoon coffee was a celebration of cleanliness. Sunday would produce the godliness. For now, it was enough that the parsonage be clean.

After an early supper, the Saturday-night-bath special rolled into high gear. Our hair was shampooed with Raleigh's. We were scrubbed clean and robed in fresh flannel nightgowns. All the shoes waited in a row for Papa's polish and buff. Mama laid out clean Sunday clothes, ready for an orderly Lord's Day.

Mama peeled potatoes for Sunday dinner, made meatballs and gravy, and cooked the carrots to cream with the peas later. A bowl of applesauce cooled. The table was stretched and a linen cloth spread, ready to cover the feet of any who needed a Sunday-noon home.

Sunday school lessons, Bibles, pennies for collection, clean handkerchiefs — all were ready for morning.

Every detail of school and play came up on the bedtime screen. Nothing was hidden from Mama. As she tucked me in, she always said, "Look at me, Margaret. Is there anything you need to tell me before we talk to God?" Knowing her secret line to God, the confessions poured out, and forgiveness followed. Sleep was sweet.

Papa sat in his study late into the night. Mama looked over the work of the day, saw that it was good, and turned out the light. If she ever did sleep, it was on Saturday night.

Sunday woke like a burst of sunshine. Papa, dressed in striped trousers, swallow-tail coat, and high starched collar, marched off to church with his Bible and songbook in hand. Mama, dressed in her made-over clothes, gathered her children, scrubbed and

numbered, unto her. We all would take our places in
the house of God. Going to church was *never* a matter of choice, but a matter of obedience. Once there,
no one moved. This was a sacred front-row seat over
which God and Papa kept a watchful eye. As hard as
I tried to concentrate my mind always wandered ahead
a few hours. I wondered how many we would have for
Sunday dinner and hoped Uncle Barney would come.

The benediction was over. I braced myself for Mr.
Meyer's Sunday morning coffee kiss. Barney was coming for dinner. It would be a good day, a day of rest
from work but not from what Mama had taught us
while working through the week. And sometimes she
taught us while laughing.

Days of grief and sorrow pass and are followed
by peace and joy; in the same way the weeks of winter
would pass and spring would send forth her buds of
promise. In her wisdom, Mother would comment,
"And summer will surely follow."

This spring, excitement stirred in the parsonage;
Mama was to be the guest speaker at the Norwegian
Baptist Women's Convention.

The sewing machine treadled through the night
as Mama made a new creation out of an old
missionary-barrel relic. The made-over dress would be
navy blue, but Mama was not color blind; her only
pair of shoes was a contrasting brown. Mama had long
ago learned how to manage on a preacher's income.
She solicited the help of the shoemaker, who dyed the
shoes to match the dress. At a rummage sale she found
a large brimmed hat. It was worn and frayed, but the
price was right: ten cents. She bought blue dye to
cover the hat's light color. After boiling and dipping
she sewed ribbons over frayed edges. Mama was

dressed, befitting the ministry: navy-blue dress with a soft lace collar, wide straw hat with ribbons, and matching navy-blue shoes, old but shining like new. Gloves and a lace handkerchief added the final touch.

The Baptist women gathered for this meeting under the open blue sky on a lovely, sunny day. String bands played, and choirs sang. The women grew eager for the highlight of the program, a reading by Ella Tweten.

Under the hot sun she stood with dignity, slender, young and beautiful. Papa would be proud. She began to speak clearly and forthrightly. But the sun refused to keep her cover-up secrets. Slowly the heat melted the hat's dye and beautiful blue streaks ran into her hair and down her forehead. The shoes reeked with the potent shoe dye, not quite dry. Mama finished her presentation with a flourish, and quietly sat down, not outwardly flustered. No one would forget the women's conference — and Mama's hat.

"A merry heart doeth good like a medicine." When the conference was over the women joined Mama in peals of laughter. Her hat became a topic for conversation for years to come.

Mama's abounding joy of living carried our family and congregation through many such crises. We learned that the joy of the Lord was our strength. Proverbs 15:15 belonged to Mama: "He that is of a merry heart hath a continual feast." The immigrants shared their sense of humor as well as their joys and sorrows.

Years later, Mama was given a gift of money (for her trip to Norway), and the accompanying note read, "To buy a hat."

six

Angels Unaware

THE TIME CAME WHEN THE FIRE began to dwindle for the Tweten immigrants in Winnipeg, and then it died. The coffee pot grew cold, but Papa and Mama left behind them a warm and mellow glow of love when Papa again felt "the call."

The Norwegian Baptist Conference asked Papa to be a missionary to the Scandinavian settlers throughout the Province of Saskatchewan.

Mama wondered how Papa would manage to travel endless miles alone, care for his clothes, and eat proper meals. However, she rested in one thing: Papa was God's servant; God never failed to care for His children.

After a painful farewell to the First Norwegian Baptist Church, the needy friends who had descended from the immigration trains, and the towering gray parsonage, Papa ushered Mama and her four children into the newly acquired Model T Ford. Mama had packed a basket of bread and sugared waffles to sustain us on the long journey.

43

Papa's Model T, provided by the Baptist Conference, was the only car he ever owned, and it never received due recognition for its service beyond the call of duty. In the days to come, this "soldier of the cross" would travel trackless space. As long as it kept wheels moving in the same direction and patiently listened to endless sermons, it was deemed worthy. Mama wondered how Papa's theological mind would remember the car needed more than words, it needed gas.

We were on our way to Saskatoon, Saskatchewan. I was ten years old, Grace was six, Gordon was four, and baby Doris was two. Papa had purchased a small house that came with monthly payments.

God and Mama would take care of the payments.

The journey grew long. The missionary and his family had already devoured their lunch. Mama was weary and wistfully mentioned how much she would enjoy a cup of coffee and a bowl of soup. Wanting to please her, when Papa saw a white cottage in an open field, he stopped to ask about a cup of coffee. There was no money for soup. While he inquired, we waited.

In just a minute Papa and a smiling Oriental emerged from the cottage. The stranger graciously invited us all to be his guests for dinner.

"Thank you," said Papa. "But we have money for only a cup of coffee."

The kind man would hear nothing of Papa's argument. He would serve us dinner.

With quiet awe we followed the charming host into a small restaurant, where we were seated at a table spread with a spotless white linen cloth. We had never been in a restaurant before. Mama sat like a queen. For once she was being served. We were the only guests present; even so, we were especially careful not to disgrace the ministry. We prompty asked a Norwegian blessing.

Our smiling host gave us his undivided attention, and he served us a *delicious* meal.

Upon leaving, each of us solemnly shook the man's hand and spoke an ever-so-polite, "Tak för matten (Thank you for food)."

"Someday, I shall return to repay you for your kindness," added Papa. "May God's richest blessing be upon you."

When we arrived at 510 Avenue J, Saskatoon, Saskatchewan, Mama's joy was boundless. The small yellow house boasted white trim and a perfect yard. "Our very own home!" she cried.

Buckets, brushes, and Fels Naptha flew into action. By the time we were finished we could have eaten off the floors. The windows shone with Canadian sunshine, and starched lace curtains framed the view.

Mama added a crowning touch to her "very own" kitchen: red linoleum (slightly damaged) purchased for one dollar. Again life flowed through Mama's kitchen.

In the corner stood the rocking chair, my place of refuge in the time of storm. When Mama needed a refuge, she just threw her apron over her head. Years later we realized her screen hid tears, but this was her world, and no one asked questions.

In another corner stood the water barrel, filled by the town water wagon, which was pulled by two horses. I loved to join the parade of skipping children who followed along and fed sugar lumps to the horses.

Behind the outhouse was an open field, a perfect garden spot. Mama's sharp eye quickly envisioned rows of bright flowers and vegetables.

The adjoining field was to become the neighborhood playground, where balls and kites could sail in the Canadian sky.

Papa unpacked his beloved books and placed them, his dearest companions, around his desk. He would soon have to travel, but now it was time for coffee. We were snugly settled into our cozy house.

The black stove glistened with polish. The coffee pot perked a welcome. Mama placed a bowl of violets she had picked on the tablecloth, set with coffee cups. Papa left his books. The children gathered for afternoon coffee and a lump of sugar, dipped in Papa's full cup.

"Mama, you have it good," he added with a bow.

Just a few days later the new neighbors came to watch Papa crank up the Model T to begin his first missionary journey. "God Will Take Care of You" became our farewell song.

Papa received only part of his salary from the Baptist Conference; he was expected to raise the rest through offerings gathered on his journeys. If the Conference had only known what Mama suspected — that the offering Papa collected at one place was given to the needy along the way to the next! But everyone was needy — including his family back home. Oatmeal became the staff of life. Mama and God had to manage. They did!

It was getting close to Christmas and we had not heard from Papa in quite some time. The cupboards held little food, and Mama's purse held no money — but worse, the soap dish was empty. Mama, desperate at such a lack, asked her Icelandic friend, Mrs. Johnson, for some soap. Having only one half-bar herself, she cut it in two. Mama had soap!

"I have only a soup bone left," added Mrs. Johnson. "That's good," said Mama. "I have a few vegetables from the grocer — there are some brown spots in them but they will be good for soup — and I have some bread. We will have a feast."

The air of festivity, songs and guitars filled the little house on Avenue J. The soup and bread seemed to multiply. Mr. Johnson led us in giving thanks to God and our joy continued late into the evening. Since the Johnsons had no children they enjoyed the four of us.

"Like Hannah of old, I have prayed for a child," Mrs. Johnson confided in Mama, "but still nothing."

"Come, we pray together," answered Mama. "God will give you the desires of your heart."

(Mrs. Johnson and Mama soon became close friends, laughing and talking over their afternoon coffee, and one year later Mr. and Mrs. Johnson dedicated their beautiful baby to God. Papa was right! God and Mama could do anything.)

Christmas Eve and still no Papa — nor offerings.

"Are you sure that God won't forget us this Christmas?" we asked.

She always answered the same way: "God never

forgets and God never fails." One old Norwegian song had become our theme song.

> Heaven and earth may pass away
> Cliffs and fjords may disappear
> But the one who trusts in God
> Knows that God's promises never fail.

Songs of faith filled the kitchen.

My memory of earlier Christmases in Winnipeg — with food and music — accented this Saskatoon holiday bleakness. Mama never wavered.

Mama had a tree brought in from the woods, and we trimmed it with our old stand-by decorations. We sang the familiar Norwegian carols, including "Yule With Its Joy." Mama presented us with new clothes made out of scraps from the missionary barrel. Mama was doing her part, if only I could have been sure God would do His.

"This is Christmas Eve," reminded Mama, "a time to rejoice and praise God for the gift of His Son. We are well. We are not hungry. We are warm. We have oatmeal, a little coffee — and sugar lumps. Papa is in God's service and God takes care of His children. Now," she ended with a flourish, "the coffee is ready."

Suddenly stomping feet hit the porch, followed by the shout of happy voices, "Merry Christmas."

"Joy to the world, the Lord is come," sang the carolers.

"Come in. Come in," exclaimed Mama. "Get warm by the fire!"

They came! Boxes of food and gifts poured into the little house. Pastor Ward, of the First Baptist Church of Saskatoon, greeted Mama. "We heard that

Pastor Tweten had not returned from his missionary journey. Please accept our love, and may God bless you all. Now we will stop for singing, and we will pray for his safe return."

I wondered how Pastor Ward knew about us since we were not members of his church, but attended a small Baptist mission near our home. The Scandinavians met in our home for weekly Bible study and prayer meeting — in their own language. At that time there was no established Norwegian church. There was a close affiliation between the Norwegian Baptist Conference and the Canadian and American Baptist Conventions.

The songs of Christmas echoed across the snow. The prayers ascended to God's throne.

As a parting gesture, Pastor Ward invited us to his home for Christmas dinner.

The boots crunched in the snow and the carolers continued singing their songs as they turned and left our walk.

Mama placed the gifts under the tree. She had already scrubbed all four of us, and we had dressed for the festivities.

Mama didn't sing "Trust and Obey" or "Faith is the Victory" without action. "If you pray for rain, you get the umbrellas out. If you pray for Christmas Eve celebration, you dress for the occasion." It was just that simple.

"Even if we have only oatmeal we dress like true Norwegians. It is not what you have that is important," she said. "It is what you believe. God never fails. That we believe!"

The table had already been covered by the white linen cloth.

Out of the boxes we all pulled prepared food, cookies, fruit, and, wonder of wonders, stick candy and nuts. Tucked in a corner we found coffee and sugar lumps. Someone had remembered our national pastime.

Suddenly boots again stomped on the porch. With a burst of joy, the door flew open!

There stood Papa!

Seated around the festive table we bowed our hearts and heads in thanksgiving to God. "Ya, Mama, I was lost in a blizzard." The story unfolded that Papa had been engulfed in a swirling Canadian storm. When he felt totally helpless, he cried out to God, "I am lost, but You know the way." A comforting Presence drew near in the blinding storm, and in a warm glow, Papa walked to the door of a hidden prairie cabin. "Ya mama, we had to shovel a path to the barn to feed the cows. We lived on oatmeal and milk until the storm passed."

On Christmas Day we sang, "Joy to the World," in the First Baptist Church, and then we were to be dinner guests in a parsonage, other than ours. Mama had dressed us girls in made-over silks and satins, trimmed with lace. My dress was blue satin, trimmed with fur. She had mended cast-off long white stockings, and reserved them for such an occasion. Our shining blond heads flaunted bright hairbows, and our little brother looked like the famous "Boy in Blue." We arrived at the parsonage, looking like fairy princesses, holding our brother in a tight grasp. The Ward children were dressed in cotton dresses and black stockings. This was our day! We were rich! Papa would not be disgraced.

Late into the night we heard Papa tell of his journeys. After we had gone to bed, Mama and Papa sat alone by the warm stove in the quiet kitchen, drinking coffee together, and catching up with time.

Many years later Papa told me that he had returned to repay the Oriental for his kindness. But he found no restaurant, and no man, just an open field. Intent on finding the man, Papa made inquiry in the community.

No Oriental had ever lived there. There had never been a restaurant, not even a house on that property.

Papa added, "To Mama and me it was such an awesome thing. We were too full of wonder to speak of it. As the years passed we became convinced that our host was an angel."

I was humbled, thinking this must have been one of God's rewards to Mama and Papa, who so freely served "angels unaware."

seven

Heart-healers

THE SCANDINAVIAN SETTLERS in the area found their
way to Mama's new house in Saskatoon, where they
gathered to share their joys and sorrows, to play the
songs of Norway on their guitars.

During the week, Norwegian services were held
in the parlor, but on Sunday we all attended the
neighborhood Canadian Baptist Mission.

The severe cold didn't keep us from enjoying the
Canadian winter wonderland. We improvised our own
toboggans and sailed into the white fairyland.

Since the river was our skating rink, we kept a
close watch over the workmen who cut huge blocks
of ice and loaded them on a sled drawn by two horses.
When the time was right, we hitched our small sleds
to the rear of the big sled and raced with the wind
across the frozen river.

Year 'round the world belonged to us, the children:
the spring with its violets in the open field, the summer and fall with thrown balls and sailing kites

against the blue sky, the wonderland of winter with frozen river and toboggan slides.

Papa seldom showed affection to Mama's children. We obeyed his stern commands — quickly! Mama was perfect; her children should be likewise. But he loved Mama in his own way. She knew his heart and understood. Understanding for us would come with the years.

One afternoon when I returned from school, my eyes saw the most wonderful thing in all the world — a piano stood in our living room.

"Margaret," announced Papa with a flourish of triumph, "You will learn to play the piano! Tomorrow I will get you a teacher. Education is not complete without music. Books and music go together."

The teacher came — a young, handsome son of another minister. I practiced!

Later I learned that Papa had sold some of his priceless books in exchange for the piano. I, too, learned to understand the heart. He gave to us the only way he knew how, and, although we didn't then understand him, I eventually saw that the piano and our music (we all learned to play the piano and we all attempted to sing) was a bridge of communication that linked Papa to his children. With the wonder of a child, he listened with approval as we filled his heart with song.

One of the many who came to 510 Avenue J was beautiful, raven-haired Sonja, dressed in chiffons and pearls. She looked like an angel as she strummed her guitar and sang the songs of Norway. I adored her — until she fell in love with my handsome music teacher. But then I caught a glimpse of how two hearts melt into one.

One day a bowl of cherries sat on the kitchen table.

I had never before seen a cherry in our house. One apple was carefully divided into six pieces. But cherries!

I rounded up my friends and we sampled the delicacy until the bowl was empty. This was my private "show and tell"!

Some time later Mama appeared in the kitchen, singing her happiness to the world. She got out the flour and shortening, ready to make the first cherry pie our oven had ever baked. With stark unbelief she picked up the empty bowl and, without saying a word, looked at me. She sank down into the rocker and pulled her apron over her head, silently weeping. Oh how I wished she had looked at the red strap on the pantry door! I left, went to the outhouse to sit – a long time. I couldn't watch Mama cry.

When I returned – oh so slowly – to the kitchen, she was cutting the brown spots out of apples, then cutting them into the waiting pie shell. Throwing my arms around her waist, I sobbed, "I'll never, never again brag or show off, never, never, never!"

She held me a long time and talked about God and forgiveness, about pride going before a fall, about God taking all things and working them together for good.

"Now we bake an apple pie – just in case somebody comes for afternoon coffee." The kitchen was alive again with Mama's singing. I set the table.

Sure enough, Mrs. Magnusen came. The apple pie was good.

Mr. Olsen, a redhead with a faraway look in his eyes, often wandered into Mama's kitchen for some good soup and rye bread. He spoke seldom, but stared into space — and drank coffee. Mama said he was very sick on the inside. He had left the big woods to work in a factory, trying to save money to bring his wife from Norway.

I had only one complaint of his frequent visits. "But, Mama, his feet smell so bad! Can't you do something?"

Do something, she did.

One cold day she suggested that Mr. Olsen warm his feet in a tub of warm water, to which Mama had added a few drops of Lysol. While he soaked his feet, she washed his stiff socks and dried them over the cookstove. She suggested that he might bring them over again with his soiled clothes — for washing day.

Mama started a ritual. Every week he came to soak his feet and pick up a clean bundle of clothes in exchange for the dirty batch he left with her. Gradually the dazed look of shock disappeared. As he drank coffee, Mama's guitar music seemed to seep into his thoughts and replace some of his pain. One day he burst into the kitchen, exploding with joy! "My Hilda comes! My Hilda comes!" That ended the foot-washing ceremony in Mama's kitchen. Who would ever have thought the way to a man's heart was through his feet. Mama understood!

Returning from one of his journeys, Papa brought home a young man, Lars.

"I found him in a barn, Mama. I think he has tuberculosis. he was vorking on a farm, but the farmer refused to pay him when he got sick. They'd agreed he would work six months before he'd be paid. He lived on oatmeal and salt pork, but was too sick to travel. I told him you could make him well." We stared open-eyed until Papa's command came, "Say hello to Lars, children."

I moved my pet rabbit off the small enclosed porch and Mama made a bed for the stranger.

Mama said he was dying from homesickness. If she cured that, God would cure the tuberculosis. We boiled his dishes and kept the little ones away from him. She fed him vegetable soup and rye bread; the songs and stories did the rest.

In the meantime she contacted his parents in Norway. They were overjoyed at the prospects of welcoming home their proud, young son, who became a prosperous citizen of Oslo. Lars had the heart-healers to thank: God and Mama.

eight

The High Button Shoes

I NEEDED SHOES! I always needed shoes! Our bank account consisted of "My God shall supply all your need." He did, but not my way!

The coming of the missionary barrel was an annual event. Every outdated relic from the gay nineties seemed to find its way into that barrel: moth-eaten furs, threadbare silks and satins, and shoes of all sizes.

I ran! I had lived through enough missionary-barrel debuts! How Mama made dresses out of those costumes I never understood. She cut apart old coats and suits and sewed beautiful coats, lined with silk. She cut off buttons and salvaged trim, and saved them for the right project. Much of the cloth she saved for quilts. We had no shortage of quilts!

"Margaret," Papa called. "We have shoes!"

That was the last thing I wanted to hear. "I'm sure they don't fit." I kept running.

"Margaret!"

I stopped. And I returned — to stare in horror at two pair of high button shoes. One pair was brown, and the other black.

"Try them on." Papa left no tone for discussion, and at times his temper moved ahead of reason.

I complained they didn't fit. I tried losing the button hook. I said they were too big. "Good," said Papa. "We'll put cotton in the toes." No one was ever sick, so it was no use even to play sick. I had to wear the shoes. No one argued with Papa.

Mama sensed my distress. Tenderly she placed her arms around me and quietly, but firmly, reminded me that we had prayed for shoes. God answered, not the way we think is best, but God heard and answered. Mama never allowed sympathy to obscure a deeper lesson.

Mama continued, "Pride is a terrible thing, Margaret. It is not so important what we put on our feet, but it *is* important where your feet go. Sometimes we have to put on hard things — like the shoes — so God can keep our feet on the right path. If you worry more about how you look than about what you are, you will have many lessons to learn. Someday you will look back and say that this was an important lesson to learn. Remember this, God always answers prayer, but not always your way. Wear your shoes with a thankful, humble heart. Shall I tell you the secret to happiness?"

"Oh yes, Mama."

As she gathered me in her arms and stroked my hair, she whispered softly, "A thankful heart, Margaret. A thankful heart."

I thought about what Mama said, but I also remembered how Papa preached about how God can move mountains if we pray, believing.

In desperation I prayed! "Dear God, the Bible says if we have faith we can move mountains. I don't need any mountains moved, I just need two pairs of shoes moved. Thank you."

I lined up the shoes, and the buttonhook, near the bedroom door, making the disappearance as easy as possible, and promptly fell asleep.

Morning came! The shoes had not gone.

"Margaret, you'll be late for Sunday school," Mama called from the kitchen.

Pulling my overshoes over my button shoes, I reluctantly left for Sunday school. Carefully wiping my feet, I started for my classroom. But despite my efforts my classmates called, "Margaret, you're dripping. You have to take off your overshoes."

Slowly, I pulled off my overshoes. There, for all the world to see, were my high button shoes. I was surrounded by silent pity.

Just then my friend Dorothy Faber walked in, carefully wiping her overshoes at the doorway. A cheerful voice called out, "Dorothy, you're dripping. Take off your overshoes."

Slowly Dorothy removed them and there, for all the world to see, were two sock-covered feet. My red-haired, frecklefaced friend had no shoes!

"Good morning girls," came the crisp English accent of our beloved Sunday school teacher. Mr. Avery, a frail, elderly, blue-eyed gentleman with white hair and goatee quietly assessed the situation.

"Dorothy, you sit here on one side of me and Margaret, you sit here on the other." Each Sunday, as we formed a large circle in our class, Mr. Avery chose two to sit beside him. It was almost like sitting near God. He had a way of making God real. No one ever wanted to be promoted to another class.

I remembered very little of what he said that morning. I only remembered what he was. I also remembered a Sunday afternoon, long before, in the Winnipeg auditorium, when I had walked down the aisle to give my heart to Jesus. Dr. R. A. Torrey had been conducting a children's crusade. I was six years old, but I knew I belonged to God.

Today I also knew I had a lesson to learn. Mama was right. Pride was a terrible thing.

Mr. Avery was saying, "With Jesus in your heart, you can do anything." I remembered that. And I still remember his love — warm and tender — as he had one arm around me, and one around Dorothy.

Dorothy and I left the classroom together. Our boots in the crunching snow created their own special echo.

We never mentioned to each other the high button shoes or the woolen socks. We each learned, what Mama would call, a lesson.

The day I gave my heart to Jesus, God gave His gift of salvation to me. The day I put on my high button shoes with humility, and not rebellion, I gave my gift to God, an obedient and thankful heart. I didn't understand it then. I understand it better now.

One day, after many years passed, a newspaper clipping came to me. Dorothy had married a minister and her poetry was a feature in her town's newspaper.

nine

Tests

"MARGARET, WAKE UP! Doris is dying!" Mama shook me out of a sound sleep, and I jumped out of bed to see three-year-old Doris suffering convulsive spasms.

After a warm mustard bath, the convulsions subsided, but the fever rose to 106 degrees. Papa and the doctor were out of town. Grace and Gordon were asleep. Mama and I were alone.

"Margaret, God's Word says, 'I will never leave thee, nor forsake thee.' Jesus is here with us, and He is the Great Physician. Come, we must pray together: Father, I hold up this child before You. I have done all I know to do. We come, in Jesus' name, to ask for healing for Doris. I put her in Your hands."

Mama continued to pray, silently, as she sponged Doris with cool water. While she rocked, she sang softly the great hymns.

A mighty fortress is our God
A bulwark never failing.

My hope is built on nothing less
Than Jesus' blood and righteousness.

Trust and obey
For there is no other way.

'Tis so sweet to trust in Jesus
Just to take Him at His Word.

We sat together through the night and sang the songs of faith — always including Mama's favorite, "Himmel og jord kan brenner," a song about the promises of God that stand when everything else fails.

When the first streaks of dawn overpowered the darkness, Doris was sleeping quietly. The fever was gone. I remembered the story of Jesus, coming to the disciples in the fourth watch of the night, and saying, "Don't be afraid. It is I." Somehow I knew that He had visited us; Mama had faced a test and I had shared in a miracle.

Another day, just as Mama was ready to go to a funeral, leaving me in charge, Gordon, age five, screamed the kind of scream that brought us all running. He had fallen down and plunged a table fork through his lip.

Mama held him in her lap, holding his lip in place with a cold cloth. We girls gathered around the rocking chair as she prayed, "This child belongs to God and Jesus never fails. Touch this mouth with Your healing power, Lord." Softly she crooned, "Saviour like a Shepherd lead us, much we need Thy tender care," then the favorite Norwegian song, "Himmel og jord kan brenner." For hours she sat, with the lip clamped shut. She continued singing softly and praying, meeting another test. I followed instructions and cared for the children — and made the coffee for Mama.

By the time dawn came peeking through the windows, Gordon's lip was perfectly healed.

What to name the new baby? Papa argued, "Solveig" (The Way of the Sun)." She would have a Norwegian name! Mama's children begged for "Joyce," an easy English name.

On the way to the city hall to register the birth of our new sister, Mama used her usual diplomacy. The registration reads, "Joyce Solveig," but she promised Papa the baby would be called Solveig. Mama's thinking was clear, "By the time she goes to school Papa will have forgotten Solveig and she will be called Joyce." A different sort of test.

When Joyce went to school a playmate came to the door one day and asked to play with Joyce.

Papa's classic question was "*Yoyce* who?" (When he reached eighty-four, Papa was still calling her "Min lilla Solveig.)

When Gordon was scheduled for nasal surgery to correct difficult breathing and to discover the source of a foul odor of unknown origin, the thought of the operation made me shudder. I'd undergone my own at home in Winnipeg. I had helped spread a blanket on the table, then listened to Papa's instruction about the can of chloroform in his hand. The next thing I had known was Papa's white face and my sore throat. Good-bye tonsils! That was in our kitchen, but Gordon was going to the hospital!

As we gathered for prayer, Mama again reminded God of His promises, that if we ask anything in His name, it shall be done. "We ask that the source of this problem be removed, and bless the doctor and the nurses," she finished.

In the next few minutes mischievous Gordon managed to get a pepper can open, and one explosive sneeze sent a button, lodged in his nasal passage, flying across the room.

Mama made sure we learned the lesson of the day: " 'My God shall supply all your need,' and today, children, God supplied surgery through a pepper can."

With God all things are possible.

We loved Saskatoon! Mama enjoyed the gardens, and the shiny house with the red linoleum, the Quaker Oats castle and fairyland of violets. We enjoyed the toboggan slides and the frozen river with the big ice sleds and horses.

People came to sing and pray, to find strength in Mama's kitchen where the coffee pot perked happily on the black cookstove. Papa traveled among the scattered settlers, and churches were organized.

At bedtime we heard songs and stories as we sat by the warm stove in our kitchen. Some songs came from Norway and told plaintive stories about the sea. One was about a little girl whose father didn't return from sea. She waited and watched by the sea to give him a birthday gift. Another song told of a crippled child who had no playmates, but he knew that when he got to heaven, the angels would play with him.

No one had to remind us to be kind to a handicapped child. Instinctively we would hug such a child and remind him how angels would play games with him in heaven. "In the meantime we will play with you."

"But Mama, why didn't the daddy come home for his birthday?" we would ask.

"Life is filled with many questions that can't be answered, children, but we must learn early to trust God and obey Him. That is one reason it is important to obey your parents. If we can't obey them, how can we obey God? Joy comes from God inside you. Even the little girl, who was sad because her daddy didn't come home, could be happy in her heart if she thought about her daddy, lost in a storm, being with Jesus. There are times when I am sad when I think about Bernice buried in New York; then I am happy when I think of her being with Jesus.

"There is a time to die, a time to be born, a time to weep, and a time to laugh. One day is never the same as the one before it or after it. But if we keep a thankful, joyful heart and learn to trust God, we will have peace all of the time."

"Mama, sing about the bird flying away."

Mama sang softly:

Flee as a bird to the mountain
Ye who are weary in sin.

"You can always fly like a bird when you think happy thoughts and believe that God answers prayer. Someday, girls, I will sew soft white nightgowns for you — out of lovely material, not rough feed sacks. On your nightgown I will embroider a bluebird — the bluebird of happiness. Always remember the bluebird, girls. Someday — not now, but someday.

Mama never lied, we knew. Over the years she repeated again and again, "Someday, I will sew you nightgowns from brand new soft white fabric. They will have on them a bluebird of happiness. Someday."

We waited. Christmas after Christmas came and went, until, finally, the boxes under the tree held the reward of Mama's lesson in hope: those promised nightgowns, lovingly sewn in the middle of our nights.

"Mama, Mama," shouted Papa. "Look at this letter. It is a call to Chicago!"

We had never seen Papa so excited! Later we learned how much he had missed New York, the libraries, subways, and universities. Little did we know that this would be Mama's supreme test.

"This is an answer to my prayer, Mama. This is God's will for us! Schools and libraries, Mama!"

Silence.

A storm was brewing.

"I am not going!" she finally said.

Shock waves swept through us — for Mama had defied Papa!

"I cannot give up this house — and my red linoleum. Chicago is full of gangsters, full of ugly noise and dirt. For the first time we have a home of our own, a garden. The children are happy. If you want schools and libraries we have some right here in Canada. I am not going!"

Late that night I overheard the same conversation. "I shall not be moved!"

Papa pleaded and argued, and then played his last card, "Mama, this is God's will!"

Defying Papa was one thing, but defying God was another.

"All right, Papa, if this is God's will, then He will have to tell me. If it involves me, I have a right to know!" Mama had stood up for herself, and she would on other occasions. We would hear that statement often in the coming years.

"Without a clear order from Him, God cannot expect me to give up the only home I have ever known. I won't move until He tells me as clearly as He told you."

"Ya, Mama, we agree! Now let us have a cup of coffee before we go to bed."

Mama sang happily as she polished her linoleum, worked in her garden, and baked her bread. God was a good God, and He wouldn't take this precious house from her. She had never been happier as she sang "Trust and obey, for there's no other way."

She placed her "fleece" before the Lord. "Now Lord, I want to obey Your will, but I must be sure it is Your will. If someone comes to buy this house, without any sign or advertisement; and if that same person wants to buy the red linoleum for what I paid for it, one dollar, then I will know it is Your will. I must be sure."

Since few houses were selling, Mama was confident no one would be looking at her small house. She sang happily.

"Excuse me, please." A pleasant lady stood in the doorway, viewing the flowers and talking to Mama. "I just passed by this darling house. Would you consider selling it?"

"Oh no," Mama answered. "I could never sell this house. Oh, just a moment. Please come in and have a cup of coffee."

"What a beautiful linoleum," the smiling lady continued. "Would you sell that linoleum to me? I always wanted a red one!"

Quietly Mama folded her hands over her starched apron. It was time for her to give up. "Yes, we will sell the house, and the red linoleum."

With her lips she said "Yes" to the smiling lady. With her heart she said yes to the will of God. God had spoken! She would trust, and she would obey!

And so it came to pass that the house on Avenue J, and the red linoleum, were sold. We were on our way to Chicago.

Five young faces pressed against the sooty windows, as the train rolled past prairies, lakes, and rivers. Tears splashed on my window, for I would never see Sivert, my first love, again.

Papa, with his open Bible on his lap, smiled jubilantly. He was heading toward his beloved seminary, libraries, elevated trains, and he was returning to the pastorate, this time at Logan Square First Norwegian Baptist Church.

Mama, with Solveig sleeping in her lap, looked out across the golden prairies, as the sunset cast an amber glow of God's love over the yellow house on Avenue J.

God did show her His will as clearly as He had shown Papa.

ten

Next Stop, Chicago!

THE LONELY TRAIN WHISTLE was a signal to the prairie children to run to the crossing and wave to the engineer of the steaming, roaring giant of the tracks. In the fields men stopped working long enough to wave, and dream, for a moment, of magical faraway places. Mothers waved their handkerchiefs and held up their babies to watch the train go by.

We, on the inside of the train, discovered a new life. Lunches out of paper bags, water from a fountain, dizzying trips to the rest room, balancing ourselves against the rythmic motion of the train, smiles among strangers all became a part of the mysterious train world.

As we counted the clicks and clacks of the rolling wheels, we were rocked to sleep on the red plush seats. The soot and cinders worried Mama more than us, for we enjoyed the trail of smoke, the whistle blasts, the jovial conductor, and all the friendly faces.

"Chicago's Union Station, next stop!" With washed faces and brushed hair, we sat stiffly beside Mama as the roar of the engine echoed within the railroad station.

A million lights danced against the dark sky. People were everywhere. I watched furtively for gangsters.

With his usual air of authority, Papa maneuvered his family and baggage into the waiting room, where we were met by the deacons of the church. No ready-made parsonage awaited us. We waited quietly while adult decisions were made and parental instructions were given: Grace, Gordon, and I (the caretaker) were to go home with the Rossings. The Knudsens took Papa and Mama with Doris and Solveig, as their guests. In the meantime a search for a flat near the church would continue.

Within a short time the family was separated, getting into two shiny cars with real glass windows. Papa's Model T, left in Canada, had featured curtains that snapped shut. Clanging streetcars, elevated trains roaring against the sky, cars heading in all directions, policemen and whistles – was this Chicago? Where did children play, when houses were piled up in rows like building blocks? It was nighttime. Why weren't children in bed? Saskatoon had a nine o'clock curfew for all children. Where were all these people going? I asked my questions in silence.

I held Grace and Gordon closer to me, wanting to protect them from this new life. A lump grew in my throat because I missed the winds of the prairie.

Papa, though, couldn't have been more delighted. Sitting in the front seat with Mr. Knudsen, he enjoyed the traffic, the sounds of the bursting city, and the lighted skyscrapers against the starless sky. Streets, familiar from his seminary days, filled him with a sense of belonging. Here were the great universities and libraries. He was coming home.

Mama, holding Doris and Solveig close, remembered her "very own" kitchen, the coffee pot, and the red linoleum. She felt the warm sun over the fields of violets, and the gentle wind of the prairie. "A few tears for my little house tonight," she thought, "but no tears for tomorrow." God had spoken. She would trust and obey. God never fails.

The car in which Mama rode pulled into the driveway of a beautiful bungalow. The Knudsens and their daughters opened their door with a Norwegian coffee welcome.

Pete Rossing's shiny car pulled into the driveway of his spacious home surrounded by verandas. Mrs. Rossing and their children, Ray and Helen, were there to greet us. I had never seen such a beautiful kitchen, with gleaming white sink and cabinets. There was no cookstove or rocking chair, and no water barrel. The table was set for "coffee" and three dishes, each containing a huge peach-half, were set before us. Taking charge of my siblings, as I'd been commanded, I promptly removed two of the dishes and proceeded to divide the one remaining peach-half in three parts. "We always divide," I said, "and then we can have peaches for two more days. We cut one orange in six pieces," I added. I wasn't too sure why the Rossings started laughing, but I joined in. When Ray showed me the pantry, lined with cans of Del Monte peaches, I realized there was no lack of supply.

"Eat the peaches children; there will be more

tomorrow," assured Mrs. Rossing.

We relished every bite.

"Come, I will help you take a bath," Mrs. Rossing suggested, after the peaches and milk.

"Oh, no," I answered quickly. "I take care of the children. No one helps us."

We were ushered into a large gleaming white bathroom. Water was filling the tub. I ran to shut off the flow, explaining that our water wagon had come only twice a week. "One barrel cost twenty five cents, so we were careful with the water. We took our baths in a round tub on Saturday night, youngest first and me last. Mama got to have clean water to wash her hair and take a bath. She let me wash her back, but I turned around when she put on her clean flannel nightgown. I brushed her hair while she sat by the fire. Since I am the oldest, I stayed up with Mama and we had coffee together on Saturday night. Papa was gone most of the time. She said that someday I would have my own clean bath water."

Mrs. Rossing assured me that there was enough warm water for the children and started to undress them.

"Oh no, I'll do that." The last thing Mama had said was that no one should see our dirty underwear, full of soot from the train. I had clean clothes in my bag and planned to wash the dirty clothes myself, not wanting to disgrace the ministry

With a soft wash cloth and a large bar of white soap, I bathed Grace and Gordon in a tub of warm water. Wrapped in a luxurious towel, I dried their golden hair and robed them in clean underwear. In a few moments they were tucked between soft blankets.

The long journey had come to an end.

Returning to the bathroom I hesitated as I looked at the grimy water. Impulsively I drained the tub. Tonight I would have my own bath water.

Here in this shining bathroom with a tub of hot water, the round tub in the kitchen was only a memory. I chuckled as I remembered the Saturday bath during which Mr. Hansen had come to the kitchen door. Mama had shoved the tub and me under the tablecloth and coaxed Mr. Hansen out of the open doorway into the parlor. Somehow I sensed that those carefree days were over. There was no way to go back for old joys; I would now have to find new joy in a new place. Mama said we carry our joy with us. I wondered if there would be another time and place when we sat with Mama in the kitchen, listening to songs and stories, while Papa traveled the prairie.

Tears splashed into the hot water; I longed for the little house on Avenue J, the rocking chair by the stove, Mama's violets on a starched tablecloth — even the red linoleum. "There is a time to weep," Mama had said. Perhaps this was the time, now, in the tub, so the sadness would all wash away. There would be tomorrow, and that would be a time to rejoice. Mama was still saying, "Remember the bluebirds — not now — but someday they will come." I would just have to keep up my hope. I drained the tub of the water and tears and quickly cleaned the bathroom. In a brown bag, the sooty underwear would wait for another day. In my long flannel nightgown, I stood tall and straight before the mirror. I was no longer a child. I was twelve years old.

I fell asleep in Helen's soft bed, dreaming of white nightgowns and bluebirds.

Within a month Papa found a six room second-floor flat within walking distance of the Logan Square church.

When the truck delivered our few household belongings, Mama was elated to see her Singer treadle sewing machine. In Canada, Papa had removed it from the truck and told the movers, "This old machine does not go!"

Mama saw things differently: "It goes!" The neighborhood children watched with delight as the sewing machine was put back on the truck, only to have Papa discard it again. Until she saw her machine in Chicago, Mama hadn't been sure what the outcome would be. At an opportune minute she had whispered to the mover, "When Papa isn't looking, please put my machine on the truck. There are some things he doesn't understand."

The movers succeeded! Papa, engrossed in the safety of his precious books, took no notice of the machine, and later Mama had it placed under an embroidered cloth, safely hidden in an obscure corner. The incident was forgotten that is — until there was another moving day.

Every nook and corner of the flat was scrubbed, just in case the former occupants weren't Norwegian. Lace curtains were placed on wooden stretchers and dried stiff with Linet starch. A rose-flowered carpet, a gift, covered the parlor floor. Lace doilies covered the backs and arms of the sofa and chair, new from the second-hand store. In front of the lace curtains stood Mama's prized possession, a small mahogany table, a gift from the lady in New York City for whom Mama had worked when she was fifteen years old. On the table was a tall, cut-glass vase, a symbol of beauty and culture, a promise of things to come. I polished the table every Saturday, always handling the vase carefully.

Home was Mama! The kitchen was the coffee pot. Security was the rocking chair. We were home! A gas stove replaced the cookstove and a small garbage burner in the kitchen gave the teakettle a permanent home. The old rocker was there, but became the zone for a battle between management and labor. Papa removed the rocker and took it to the basement. "Mama, people in Chicago don't have rocking chairs in the kitchen." With Papa no negotiating table existed. Mama knew when to surrender – but only for a season. After a few days she said, "Children it is time to get the rocking chair." Labor took over, and the chair was hauled up two flights of stairs – that is, until Papa discovered the chair again (perhaps months later) and took it back to the basement. Mama waited for the right moment. It returned!

Uncle Barney's dramatic appearance to the second-floor flat prompted shouts of unrestrained joy from all of us children.

"Without the most beautiful girls in the world, Canada lost its charm," he announced with a mock bow. "Besides, no one makes coffee like Mama." Winking at her, he said, "I need to watch over the pastor in this wicked city. He is oblivious to the ways of the world." Grabbing us all in his arms he added, "These Tweten girls are too pretty to turn loose in this town, so I decided that old Barney had better head for Chicago." I never quite knew how oblivious or naive Papa was. One day when I had WLS tuned in on the radio and was listening to their barn dance, I told Papa I was listening to Moody Bible Institute's Radio station. Papa said, "You know, Mama, Moody is getting kinda vorldly."

Tonight the kitchen was warm with laughter. Barney strummed his mandolin while Papa tapped his foot. Mama turned out the hot loaves of rye bread to cool with a promise that I could have both end slices.

Just my girls and me,
And Solveig makes three;
We're happy in Mama's kitchen.

"More, Barney, more!" we shouted.

Barney sang, "I'm coming back to you, my hula hu," then a plaintive song about the fisherman's daughter. The words were never the same. He made them up as he went along. When he played and sang a Norwegian song Mama and Papa, misty-eyed, joined in. We, too, saw the fjords and cliffs and the midnight sun.

Mama poured coffee, and sliced the hot bread, while Papa and Barney roared with laughter over the same Norwegian jokes. This was Mama's moment. "Barney, would you get my rocking chair out of the basement, please?" She poured the second cup of coffee and patted Papa on the cheek.

Papa impulsively grabbed her, pulled her onto his lap, and kissed her. "Ya, Barney, let's get Mama's rocking chair!"

Sunday was Papa's day. He arose at dawn, singing, "Tille Nu Pa Sundags Morgen (Early Now on Sunday Morning)." Pacing back and forth in the parlor he read aloud the Scripture and preached to the rising sun.

In the kitchen, Mama made last minutes preparations for Sunday dinner. The table had been set the night before, and all was in order for the Lord's Day.

In God's house, Papa, elegant in his dignity, stood up to announce the opening hymn, "Lover den Herre, den mektige Konge (Praise Ye the Lord the Almighty King)."

Mama and her children sat quietly, with folded hands in reverent awe, for we were at home, in Logan Square Norwegian Baptist Church, in Chicago.

Tuesday night was string band practice. Some of the musicians rode two hours on the elevated trains and street cars to attend. Mama played the guitar, but couldn't read music, so someone wrote out the chords for her. After decisions were made on Norwegian or English songs and the instruments were tuned, only a limited time remained for practice.

The highlight of the Sunday evening service was Papa announcing, "Now we will hear from the string band." Together, they arose and inched their way through the crowded pews, down the aisle, to the string band table. It never occurred to them to be seated before the service. This was their moment of glory! After a long week of service to others in an English-speaking society, this service belonged uniquely to them. This was their home, their church, and these were their songs. Sometimes they started in broken English, but ended up in Norwegian. No one but the very young seemed to mind, and we could never understand why visiting Americans requested songs from the string band.

Mr. Lundaman played the violin and led the string band with his bow. One evening, with great enthusiasm, he conducted, "Han Skal Åpne Perla Porten

(He the Pearly Gates Will Open)" and the string band played it at least six times. With a flourish he finished and we fully expected the gates to open — that moment.

Mr. Nilsen played the mandolin, and when the pearly gates opened for him one Christmas Eve, the young and old mourned for the happy Norwegian and his mandolin.

Hans played the zither, and that seemed to be the only time the loneliness left him. There were many guitars, too, strumming in unison to Mr. Lundaman's violin solos.

One of Papa's devoted converts gave me a ten-stringed instrument, played like a ukelele. Amid the giggles of my friends, I joined the march down the aisle, with the "old" Norwegians. I would rather have died, but one look from Papa sent me on my way. No one disgraced the ministry by refusing to serve the Lord.

Papa's reverential awe of eloquent theologians brought biblical scholars to the church on Logan Square.

When Dr. James M. Gray, minister in the Reformed Episcopal church and the president of the Moody Bible Institute in Chicago, was escorted to the platform one memorable Sunday, the congregation stood to express their gratitude to this distinguished guest. The church was packed! The string band played. The choir sang. The congregation joined in unison: "A mighty fortress is our God." Again, some sang in Norwegian, others in English. It didn't matter. This was their church, and their God had come with them to the new land. Watching Dr. Gray's face, I somehow knew he understood.

Accompanying Dr. Gray was a Moody Bible Institute radio station soloist, who in his beautiful tenor voice sang, "What shall I give Thee, Master?" When he concluded the song and turned to be seated, he was interrupted by a small Norwegian grandmother, standing to her feet, "Young man, sing that song vun more time, it vas such a blessing." The tenor returned and sang to the grandmother. When he had finished, she again stood, said, "T'ank you," and sat down. Dr. Gray smiled. After all this was her church. And Papa understood.

Dr. Gray, so dignified with his silver hair and silver beard, stood quietly behind Papa's pulpit. With eloquent dignity he opened the Bible and spoke. Papa's expression reflected the heart of his congregation. The people nodded to each other. This godly man might not be Norwegian, but he knew their God. When he closed the Bible in conclusion, the church stood as one, to honor the man of God who shared his faith with them.

Outside, the Chicago traffic rumbled on, while inside the church, the guest and the Norwegian people sang together:

Blest be the tie that binds
Our hearts in Christian love.

eleven

The Picnic

DURING THE WARM SUMMER MONTHS Mama's Monday wash was on the line early. White sheets, embroidered pillow cases, linen tablecloths, and napkins whipped in the morning breeze. Papa's Sunday shirt bowed stiffly, while underwear clung together in a less conspicuous place. Mama's intimate apparel, including a boned corset, with laces, hung in seclusion on the porch. Towels were clipped together according to size, while the Chicago wind rattled through thirty-five starched dresses, the aprons, and the embroidered luncheon cloths used for afternoon coffee. The sun filtered through the hazy day.

Tuesday we would tend the basket of ironing, but Monday was picnic day. Papa, relaxing from the strenuous "day of rest," packed his Bible and one of Spurgeon's books and hurried everyone along in his usual, impatient manner. For him the shortest distance between two points was *action*. We moved! The house had been put in order, and the food had been prepared. Before 10 A.M. we were standing on the corner of Wrightwood and Kimball, waiting for the Diversey Avenue bus. We hoped there would be seats.

One large bag contained meatballs and gravy in a covered kettle, wrapped in towels to stay warm. Another bag included waffles with melted butter and sugar, also wrapped in a towel. Rye bread, cheese, jam and cookies and cake filled a third container. Dishes and tablecloth went into still another bag. Mama's mending was included with jars of milk and coffee. Bathing suits were tucked into empty places.

Papa, holding Joyce Solveig and his books in one arm, the meatballs in the other hand, managed to steer Mama and her children, who were holding blankets, a pillow, and the bags, into the bus. The expressionless bus driver patiently counted the seven fares. The aroma of the meatballs filled the bus. With a sigh of relief, the driver finally called out, "Diversey Beach," and Mama counted heads and bags, accounting for all that she had meant to bring.

We promptly forgot the second-floor flat and the Chicago heat when we saw the waves rolling in on the shores of Lake Michigan. A blanket cabana facilitated our speedy change into swim suits. Papa walked the shoreline, reading Spurgeon aloud, while we raced into the waves. Wistfully, Mama looked across the water and remembered her home by the sea, the cliffs and fjords, her land of the midnight sun. When the lake breeze blew through her brown hair she felt again the wind of the prairie and remembered her very own house. With a settled sigh, she picked up her mending bag and slipped the wooden egg into the toe of another needy stocking. A poetry book propped up before her, her darning needle flew back and forth, powered by her determined fingers. While she worked, the beauty of words refreshed her soul.

By noon, Papa wandered back from his rendezvous with Spurgeon and signaled his dripping enthusiastic brood to follow him. (We always suspected that he knew more about Spurgeon than he did about any of us.)

The starched tablecloth was spread, and napkins, made out of feed sacks and personalized by varied embroidery thread, were set out. With dignity we asked the Norwegian blessing and then Mama served meatballs and gravy over boiled potatoes and carrots. Thin slices of buttered rye bread supplemented the menu. Sponge cake and a part of an apple finished the meal off. The Good Humor ice cream cart jingled in the background, but there was no need to look longingly at the chocolate-covered delights. The pennies had been counted out to cover the bus fare. We drank our fill from and washed the dishes in the water fountain.

"For everything there is a season," and now it was time to rest. In the midst of a noisy beach, Mama cradled Joyce Solveig in her arm and took her usual nap. Doris and Gordon sat quietly, looking at a book, while Papa read his Bible. Grace and I watched the crowded beach.

A mother, screaming at her children, waved frantically, "No, Sammy, no, you don't wee in the water." She turned to her neighbor, "So I told him already, but do kids listen? Rebecca, come back. Don't drink the water. Sammy weed already!" She turned to her friend on the next blanket, "A little peace I come to get, and what do I have? A headache and indigestion! My mother should know! Jake? What does he know? He says 'Today, your papa takes you and Mama to the beach, and I'll pick you up in a car after work.' Rebecca! Rebecca! Lifeguard, lifeguard, help! My Becky is drowned already! You know what else Jake says? 'A cleaning woman you have no less.' In my coffin they'll see me."

Mama sat up, smiling, "That was a good nap."

"Ya, mama, but now it is time for coffee." Out of one of the bags came a jar of coffee, still warm from towel wrappings, and a sugar lump. There was time for another splash, while Papa walked the beach — but only after a trip to the rest rooms. No one disgraced the ministry, in or out of the water.

Suppertime came too soon. A quick change out of bathing suits brought us all to the spread table again. Meatball sandwiches, warm waffles with sugar, cookies and apples emptied the bags and filled the table. Nothing was left. Washed dishes were packed away, so were the blankets, suits, and towels. Mama tucked away her mending and another poem in her memory. Traffic was less congested; soon the buses would be empty. The waves splashed over the rocks and sand and from the bus windows we watched the sun slip behind skyscrapers, saying goodnight to the windy city. The bus stopped.

Papa led the way, up to the second-floor flat. Everyone helped to get the clothes off the line and then, in the tub, the children washed off the sand. I helped Mama sprinkle clothes for tomorrow's ironing. Papa played the piano and, with his usual gusto, sang "Standing on the Promises." While Mama put on the coffee pot, I took my bath and slipped into my side of the bed. Grace slept by the wall, Doris in the middle, and I, being the oldest, slept on the edge. I could wash out the sand of Diversey Beach, but I could never erase the memories. The music stopped, for coffee was ready. I fell asleep thinking how rich we were. Some people had vacations once a year. We had one every week of the summer: the Monday picnic.

twelve

Growing Up

To the Norwegian people the red brick walls of the church on the Square were not walls made of stone. They were walls built out of love in years of loneliness, comfort in hours of sorrow, and hope in moments of despair. To the young, the walls contained golden dreams of tomorrow and moonlight and roses of romance.

No one walked alone! The young and the old together dreamed the impossible dream, and with heads held high, their faith could bear the most unbearable of sorrows. Their answer to death was "I am the resurrection and the life, he that believeth in Me, though he were dead, yet shall he live (John 11:25)." The answer to the dark days of the Great Depression was, "But my God shall supply all your need according to His riches in glory by Christ Jesus (Philippians 4:19)." The answer to loneliness was, "I will never leave thee, nor forsake thee (Hebrews 13:5)." During difficult periods of change in a new land the answer was, "Jesus Christ the same yesterday, and today, and for ever (Hebrews 13:8)" and "For ever, O Lord, Thy word is settled in heaven (Psalm 119:89)." The answer to fear was, "Fear thou not; for I am with thee: be not dismayed; for I am thy God: I will strengthen thee; yea, I will help thee; yea, I will uphold thee with the right hand of My righteousness (Isaiah 41:10)."

The answer to youth who were rebelling against the old Norwegian ways was the apostle Paul's warning to Timothy: Forget not the ones who taught you, your mother and grandmother.

Within the walls of home and church stood the protective laws of Moses. The "Thou shalt nots" were a wall stronger than stone, more valued than gold.

Discipline of the will was the sun and rain that nurtured the seeds of obedience and trust planted in my heart.

During my high school days, Eleanor Holby, Eleanor Knudsen, Coreen Nelson, and I were always together. Coreen's mother had made me a beautiful blue silk dress for my first Christmas in Chicago. Mr. Holby had packed Mrs. Wiberg's World Vild Girls into his seven-passenger Studebaker. This memorable trip was to Williams Bay, Wisconsin, with Papa's parting words, "No svimming on Sunday." Mama and the treadle machine produced a proper bathing suit "to cover." I shudder to remember how covered I was.

Then there was the young peoples' excursion to the sand dunes of Lake Michigan, near Gary, Indiana. Everyone left early in the morning, but Rainey Gotaas, a preacher's son, and I couldn't leave until after church service. Rainey would drive and Mama said I should sit in the back seat. Papa said I should sit in the front seat, but not too close. Mama put the watermelon between us. All this in full view of Papa's church. Everyone waved as Rainey's car sputtered off to a good start.

As we neared the sand dunes, the car broke down, the horn kept blowing, and we couldn't find the young people and worse, the food! We walked miles in search of our crowd and finally settled for a hot watermelon picnic. Maybe Mama was right. She didn't believe in picnics on Sunday. Rainey searched his pockets and came up with enough fare to catch the midnight train home. In the meantime the young people were back to the evening service and every head watched for the missing strays. Papa and the deacons almost called an emergency session, but we made it home – hot, tired and sick from too much watermelon.

About this time Jeanelle, the baby, was born. How I resented Mama *so old*, having a baby! She was thirty-eight! It was crowded *enough* in our second floor cold-water flat. A new baby wasn't an exciting thought for a fifteen-year-old sister. Mama had whispered to our nurse friend, Leona, "Help Margaret." In the quiet of the night Leona talked to me about families, births, and life. She talked about attitudes and understanding, and when she was finished I was weeping in Mama's room, "I'm sorry, and I'll do all I can to help you."

For years I shivered whenever I relived the night one-month-old baby Jeanelle was dying of pneumonia. Dr. Thornton patted Mama on the shoulder. "Mama, you have five. Be ready to give this one back to God, for she can't live through the night." I could see it all again, the tiny blue form gasping for air.

That's when Leona arrived! "We've been through too much having this baby — and she will live!" She rubbed Jeanelle with warm olive oil, and sucked the mucus out of her throat. I prayed for God to forgive me for not wanting this baby, and now I wanted her to live more than anything else in the world. We prayed, Leona rubbed. By morning Jeanelle was warm and pink. God had saved His child.

To get us through depression days, Mama found a cheaper first-floor, cold-water flat on Ridgeway Avenue. We were grateful for the convenience of the first floor, but how we missed the larger rooms of the other flat. To help out with expenses I worked, after school and on Saturdays, at the National Tea Company grocery store.

The cold water flat was just that — cold! One stove stood in the dining room, and a garbage burner stood in the kitchen. A gas pilot flame heated the water tank in the kitchen.

It was a comforting sound to hear Papa shake the stoves, even if it was 5 A.M. That meant an extra hour of sleep for me, snuggled under Mama's quilt beside Doris and Grace.

In his long flannel nightshirt Papa shook the stove with a vengeance and sang "Standing on the Promises." Mama sent loaves of bread as a peace offering to the neighbors, who promptly forgave Papa's morning concert. Besides they were already up, shaking their own stoves.

Before long I heard the crackle of burning wood and fell asleep. At 6 A.M. Papa called me, and I dressed quickly in the cold room. Papa was quietly reading his Bible, rocking gently in the big rocker by the stove.

On the table was a cup of hot cocoa and six slices of hot buttered oven toast. He kept reading. No one disturbed Papa.

At 6:45 I left for high school, for class began at 7:30, and I had three miles to walk. Papa's words were, "Ya, Margaret, study hard and button your coat good." I answered a polite, "Takk for maten (Thanks for food)," kissed him on the cheek and left to meet my girl friend, who had made her own breakfast and eaten it alone. We carried our books and a bag of lunch. I had four slices of rye bread and cheese. We drank from the water fountain, but on Friday I had five cents for a Hershey bar. Life was good.

Years passed before I realized that Papa had communicated his love in his own way — a warm kitchen, toast and cocoa, giving Mama an extra hour of sleep before the younger children had to get up. I wish I had said more than "Takk for maten." Some day, I will!

On Saturdays I gave Mama my week's pay: four-dollars-worth of groceries. Hamburger was two pounds for twenty-five cents. Added to that were free soup bones and half-price vegetables at closing time. After surgery performed by Mama, apples, minus their brown spots, made good applesauce. I brought home day-old bakery rolls, potatoes, carrots, coffee, oatmeal, and Jello-O.

Mama's meatballs had become famous, and no one could duplicate them — not even her daughters. She learned the secret of kneading bread crumbs into two pounds of hamburger, ground twice. She added spices and onions until the consistency was perfect. Placing them in a hot skillet, Mama browned the meatballs slowly and evenly. A dark gravy bubbled forth when the flour browned slowly and potato water was added gradually. She placed the meatballs into the gravy and simmered them slowly. Mashed potatoes, molded and decorated with chopped parsley, were served in a beautiful dish. Creamed carrots and peas topped off the best of meals.

As always, homemade rye bread made its way from the oven to the table. And for dessert — prune whip, sponge cake, or devil's-food cake. The golden coffee poured from the never-empty pot, as cups and hearts were filled with love.

But when I quit work to start nurses' training, Mama missed the "extras" my job had given her. Her menu made use of the most basic of basics.

On one afternoon off from nurses' training, I cut through Humboldt Park to walk about four miles to Mama's kitchen. Over a cup of coffee I recounted the events of the week, class activity, and probationary duty. I described my friends, Betty Schweitzer (another preacher's daughter) and my affluent roommate, Hertha Petersen. Hertha was in love with a chicken farmer and sang "Speak to Me of Love" until all the dormitory radios were tuned up full volume to accompany her. Betty was undoubtedly the most loving, gentle friend imaginable. When asked what she wanted to become, her soft brown eyes opened wide, "A mother, of course."

The kitchen was warm. The coffee pot perked happily. Jeanelle, the baby and beloved pet of the family, sat on my lap. I doubted that she ever had a spanking. By the time she had been born Papa was worn out, and the strap and red pepper were long forgotten.

The bread was warm, spread with melted butter. Mama slipped me the end slices because I was "special." I was home.

"Tell Margaret about the baloney." Grace, who was now the oldest at home, prodded Mama to tell me the "story of the week." Barney chuckled as the story emerged.

A few days earlier Mama had looked in her cupboard and found it nearly bare. Undaunted, she proceeded to dice potatoes for her well-known dish of creamed potatoes. She stirred up a thick sauce, seasoned with spices, onions, and parsley; then she plopped in the cooked potatoes. "Lord, it would be so nice to have ten-cents-worth of baloney to fry just a taste to spruce up these potatoes."

In the meantime, Barney, who had been walking along the street, pondering the depression and lack of work suddenly fingered a dime that had been hiding in the seam of his pants pocket. Inspiration struck! "That is just enough for baloney," he thought.

He traded his dime for some meat and hurried to Mama's kitchen.

What a good story, and so typical of God's answers to Mama's prayers. I had gone off to nursing school and left her, but God hadn't. He was as much with her as He was with me, across town.

I returned to the dormitory before 10 P.M. Lights were out at 10:30. After we heard the footsteps of Miss Abrahamson, the night supervisor, pass our door, Hertha turned on her radio and tuned in to Wayne King's "The Waltz You Saved for Me." Mama might not approve, but it was Hertha's doing, not mine. Hertha dreamed of her chicken farmer, and I rode the tractor with Sivert, or galloped across the prairie with the wind. Out of the mist walked Barney carrying ten-cents-worth of baloney to Mama.

thirteen

Voted Out

THE PRE-DAWN STILLNESS WAS BROKEN by the street sounds of the rumbling milk wagon and it's horses' clicking hoofs. The milkman made friendly sounds, the juggling of glass milk bottles. I liked knowing that someone was awake with us, the nurses on the night watch.

I had a moment to catch my breath, the lull before the onslaught of washbasins and bedpans. I stepped out on the fire escape to watch the windy city uncurl like a sleeping cat. It stretched, yawned, and stepped into a new day.

My nurses's training at the Norwegian American Hospital was drawing to a close. I had been assured a position as staff nurse at the Lutheran Deaconess Hospital. My friend, Gladys Thompson, whom I had met at Cook County Hospital during the six-month special training course had arranged an interview with Sister Regina. I could hardly wait to pay back to Mama the three hundred dollars she had loaned me. She had cashed in an insurance policy so I could buy books and uniforms. How fast the years had gone!

"Well, Florence Nightingale, a penny for your thoughts." Hertha, my roommate, joined me with a cup of coffee and quietly we watched the horses below. Hertha was probably remembering her numerous romances: but I was taken back to the first night in the nurses' dormitory.

I could still feel the aloneness of a spacious empty room, with twin beds, two dressers, two desks, and a clothes closet. Mama and Leona had accompanied me on the street car, with all my possessions in one box. A wrist watch, with a second hand, had been presented to me by the Young People's Society. Nels Olsen had wrapped it in a huge box, and after layers of paper there was my shiny watch. How I loved the young people of Papa's church. They gave me gifts of underclothes, stationery, handkerchiefs, and one pair of silk hose from Leona. There was a beautiful plaque containing the Florence Nightingale pledge from Pearl Olsen. From a shy, retarded girl was another beautiful plaque with the poem by Annie Johnson Flint — "He Giveth More Grace."

Beautiful white-haired Mrs. Knight had given me my first new brown store-bought coat. At the same time Leona had bought my first pair of high-heeled shoes and store-bought dress. I was rich with gifts of love.

I continued to unpack my treasures, and there on the bottom, wrapped in wax paper, was a box of homemade fudge from Grace. A wave of homesickness engulfed me for I could see Grace, Gordon, Doris, Joyce and Jeanelle helping (and tasting) the surprise. Home was where Grace, Doris, and I slept in one bed, where we each had one dresser drawer. Gordon slept on a couch in the dining room. Joyce and Jeanelle stayed close to Mama.

The horses were clopping in the distance. Our coffee cups were empty. With a sigh Hertha gave my arm a tug. "Come on Florence Nightingale. Let's get back to work!" Sailing down the long hall we bumped into Dr. Thornton making his early (4-7 A.M.) rounds.

"Here, take this." Our beloved physician and friend tossed oranges to us tired nurses. Some mornings he would appear with a bag of grapefruit on his back. His Abe Lincoln form ambled down the hall to dole out the pink, blue, and white pills he kept in his pocket. No rules controlled him, the rugged individualist, psychiatrist, lawyer, world traveler, lecturer — and friend.

At one time he wanted to take my brother Gordon under his domain and educate him to be a doctor. Papa's Norwegian pride loomed like a mountainous obstacle course. (He probably wanted his son to be a minister.) The compassionate heart of Dr. Thornton understood not only Papa, but the true value of his son.

Sometimes Mama would find a bag of potatoes and a big fish wrapped in paper on her back porch. That night we would feast on fish and parsley potatoes with melted butter. Or before dawn we might hear a retreating footstep, and we would find a bag of oranges or grapefruit on the porch. And we would know Dr. Thornton had been there.

One night, near the end of our term, while Hertha and I were studying for our biology exam, I was called to the dormitory phone.

"Margaret, this is Grace." There was a momentous pause. "Papa has been voted out!"

No one but a preacher's kid can know the devastating effect of the phrase "voted out." By this time I had deep respect for those denominations that gracefully moved their pastors and protected parsonage families from the trauma of being voted out. The democratic process sounded good, but a negative majority (and the vote could be *so* close) could leave unsightly scars on the church's members and on the pastor's family.

Unable to share the family disgrace with anyone, I went to class and failed the biology exam for which I was well-prepared. Sensing that something was wrong, my professor arranged for a make-up exam and a trip home.

Making my way through Humboldt Park, I tried to figure out what could have gone wrong with Papa's call. In my mind the ministry had somehow been disgraced. For ten years we had been a church family. How could this happen to us? I walked faster. I had to get home. They needed me!

I arrived home to find Mama in a crisp starched apron, putting on the coffee pot. She was singing "The trials of life will seem nothing, when we get to the end of the way." Gathering her in my arms I breathed in the fragrance of Palmolive soap and starch. Into my soul I breathed the fragrance of faith.

The bread was warm, just out of the oven. Barney and Leona were there. Papa had locked himself in the study. The younger children busied themselves with their duties. When Mama casually announced, "Come, Papa, coffee is ready," he emerged from behind the closed door with a gracious bow. "So Margaret has honored us with her presence," he commented, obviously he was pleased I had come.

Leona was furious, reporting life as she saw it: "They wanted an American pastor, one more geared to the changing times."

Barney chuckled, "You should have heard Mrs. Andreason tell about Papa bringing Mama's homemade soup to her at Cook County Hospital. 'He said to me, "Come, drink Mama's soup," and he fed me from a jar wrapped in a towel to stay warm. "You will get well. We are praying," and he spooned the warm soup into my mouth.' Poor Anna just shook her head and then said, 'That wonderful man. The police thought I was crazy—but he said I was Norwegian.' "

Some had wondered where they would go for Sunday dinner. And Barney continued, "Your papa said nothing. But you should have heard your mama. She waited until after the voting and then stood up. 'I will tell you a story,' she said. And your mama told about the yellow house on Avenue J and the red linoleum — 'Then I will go to Chicago. When God spoke I had to obey,' she said. 'I know God led us here for these ten wonderful years, and I know God never fails. He will have another place for His servant. I love this church. I love everyone and will continue to worship the Lord in this place. God bless you all.' "

"What will you do now?" I asked.

Mama's answer never changed. "God never fails, but it will be interesting to see how He works this one out. But now we have coffee."

Over the next few weeks Papa retreated to the libraries, too dazed to face the situation. God and

Mama would have to work it out.

They did!

Grace was employed by the John Anderson Publishing Company, where the Scandinavian newspaper was published. At twelve dollars a week she had been hired as Lillie Olsen's assistant. (To date Lillie Olsen is still a faithful member of Papa's former church.) Gordon started his day at 4 A.M. with a paper route. He cleaned the basement for his music teacher to pay for his violin lessons. When he held out his grubby hand, offering his first fifty cents to the family budget his face shone with pride. Papa, who lashed out at trivial episodes in his children's lives, saw the grubby hand. Mama saw the giving heart. God saw the seeds of rebellion being sown by a father's rejection of his son's true worth. Doris assumed responsibility in the home. Joyce watched over Jeanelle.

I waited for graduation.

One of the quiet, lonely ones whom Mama had befriended through the years came forward timidly with "I find vork for you in River Forest." So it came to pass that Mama became a cleaning maid again. Through the years I have often wondered if the house Mama cleaned has been singularly blessed by having had an "angel unaware" scrub its floors.

Papa attended the various large churches on Sunday morning, just another face in the crowd. Mama and her children continued to attend the church on the Square, but, without Papa, it was never the same.

Occasionally Papa received invitations to preach. On one such Sunday he took the wrong street car, but didn't realize it until he was too late for the service. In despair he continued riding for hours, too ashamed to return home or contact the pastor of the church. A phone call from the pastor prepared Mama, who waited for him with a soothing hot cup of coffee. Until he returned Mama prayed quietly.

While Papa retreated into his study and the libraries, life went on for Mama and her children. I was preparing for graduation, and for a brief period Papa joined in the festivities and proudly gave the invocation on graduation day. My student "stripes" (those tell-tale uniforms) were packed away, and I reported for full-fledged duty at the Lutheran Deaconess Hospital.

One day Papa received an invitation to conduct tent meetings in Wisconsin. With faith renewed, Mama packed him off on a rewarding summer trip. When he returned, a call awaited him. The First Norwegian Baptist Church, Fifty-seventh Street, Brooklyn, New York, wanted Papa to be their leader.

Grace and I watched the train slowly pull away from the Chicago station. In the midst of elevated trains, clanging street cars and rushing people, we were suddenly alone. Home was slipping down the tracks toward Brooklyn. The cold-water flat on Ridgeway Avenue stood empty.

Then the day came when Grace boarded another train and followed them to New York.

My world was never the same; I then had to depend only on God, who became my home — and who would never "vote me out."

fourteen

Brooklyn, America

THE TRAIN WHEELS CLICKED and clacked over the rails. Villages and fields were discarding drab winter covering for bursts of color and splashes of rain and sun. It was April, 1938. The New York Central was leaving Chicago behind, delivering a homesick daughter to New York for a family visit.

Again I relived the train ride from Canada and longed for the wind of the prairie and for a time that would be no more. Settling back into the plush seats, I rolled with the motion of the train as scenes from the past rolled together like the fields and towns outside my hazy window.

I chuckled to myself as I remembered a handsome minister from Norway, and his "prayer meeting" with a farmer's daughter. I had inadvertently stumbled into the room in the middle of a not-so-holy kiss. One word to Mama sent an S.O.S. to Norway, and the secret code between wives resulted in action. Sooner than expected, the minister's adorable wife arrived on the scene. The curly-haired, saucy-eyed wife charmed her way into the hearts of everyone, especially Mama. The wife never made reference to the reason for the surprise visit, except to let the farmer's daughter know how much the wife had missed her charming husband. Chuckling over a cup of coffee, Mama and the wife agreed: "You do your part, God will do the rest." The subdued husband and his sparkling wife blended together like coffee and cream. When Papa spoke highly of that devoted couple, Mama smiled over her coffee cup.

"There are some things you tell, and some things you don't tell," Mama had said to me when I told her of my abrupt interruption of the hungry kiss. Her look told me that I had been entrusted with a secret — that we were to keep this as ours.

I wondered what had happened to another girl, Karen, who had loved Lars, a tall curly-haired immigrant. Out of a sense of obligation, Lars had married Bertha, a shy childhood friend from Norway. I remember Karen's sad face in the crowd at the wedding. Coming down the aisle Lars met Karen's eyes. I often wondered what Mama said to Karen after the wedding, when Mama stroked her soft golden hair and whispered in her ear. Perhaps she said, "Love suffers long and is kind." Karen folded her love like a tent, and let it slip silently into the mist of memories. She grieved quietly, then moved away.

There was another night in Canada when Papa took a young husband aside and urged him to take his beautiful wife away from the source of a problem — a handsome young man from Norway, who loved her. Mama took the wife aside. No one but those two knew what was shared over afternoon coffee. The wife returned her loyalty to her rightful lover, her husband. Years later Papa found them in another town, happy and prosperous. "We never make a mistake to do what is right in God's sight. God honors obedience," Mama had reminded me.

The conductor interrupted my thoughts with a cheerful, "Hope you are enjoying the trip; the dining car is open."

"Thank you, I am enjoying the trip and would love a cup of coffee."

The white linen cloth, polished silver, and starched porter reminded me of home. I soon forgot the menu, but the memory of people in red plush seats, dignified, starched porters carrying white linen napkins, the sound of cups and silver, and a current of conversation between strangers still blend in my mind — a page out of another time. Through smoky windows the world rushed by, and with it that mystical girl and boy land fled, never to return. Just as the landscape of rivers, trees, villages and people, clouds, and sky blended into one moving picture, so the scenes from home blended into one picture — Mama. That must be why Papa needs her so desperately, I thought. She is his home, his roots, his source of life and meaning, for she continually directs his steps back to faith in God. "God entrusted Papa to me," she would say. "God knew I would love him, care for him, believe in him — and always understand him. In turn God made a promise to me — that all my children shall be taught of the Lord. God never fails."

I saw the endless stream of lonely ones that Papa brought to Mama, the universal mother. Since she was his harbor, she could harbor all the human driftwood he found along the shore. To every problem there was one answer: "God and Mama." To every grief, one solace: "Mama will understand." God had given him someone special and he had to share her with the world.

There was that Wednesday service after which the visiting speaker came home to spend the night. While we girls were setting out our floor pallets, Mama asked the gentle white-haired Pastor Anderson what he would like to eat before retiring. "Oyster stew," he announced confidently. We gasped! No one had seen an oyster in our house, much less eaten one.

Without flinching, Mama went to the kitchen and toasted her homemade bread, cut pieces in small squares, and poured scalded milk over the toast. Seasoned with salt, pepper, and butter, she placed a china bowl full of her "oyster stew" before the elderly guest.

"This is the best oyster stew I have ever eaten," he boasted on Mama's behalf. "Now I would like a cup of silver tea." Into a fine, china cup Mama poured boiling water, with cream and sugar: her own concoction for children and the elderly. Pastor Anderson enjoyed his "silver tea" while Papa drank his coffee. I still remember the look of admiration and wonder when Papa's eyes met Mama's laughing eyes. He was remembering her maxim: "It is not the problems, but how you meet them that counts. You do your part and God will do the rest — even in making oyster stew."

I wondered if I would be able to do my part as well as she had. My marriage to Harold Jensen (a Dane who knew how to celebrate a Norwegian Christmas) was fast approaching. Leona and Monroe were in the Ozark Mountains of Arkansas, doing missionary work under the American Sunday School

Union. Barney had married Mildred, his anchor in the time of storm. The fires of romance and dreaming had burned out, at least for a time, and Barney had settled into a comfortable marriage of stability and companionship. I toyed with the idea of moving to New York, to be near my family, but I had made a commitment. With it came the knowledge that this bird couldn't return to the nest. One by one Mama's children would learn to fly. As the sentimental eldest I sighed for a time that would never be again – the simple days of childhood when Mama had been able to fix anything and everything.

"Grand Central Station!" Like a snorting horse the train thundered into the station. On the platform stood Papa, handsome, as always, and impatient to get me home to Mama and a cup of coffee. Happy and talkative, he seemed pleased to have his first-born again under his roof.

"Come to New York, Margaret! You will love it. There is so much to see. Tomorrow I'll take you to the library, then to Carnegie Hall where Grace takes her piano lessons. You must see it all, the Statue of Liberty, the harbor and ferry boats, the great churches, Wall Street, Fifth Avenue, Radio City, Coney Island, Brooklyn and the church on Fifty-seventh Street. You will love the people. You still want to marry a Dane? Oh ya, Harold is fine – could be taken for Norwegian. Come, run and we catch the subway." Even the suitcase couldn't slow him down until we were seated, breathless, on the subway heading to Brooklyn. He continued, "Mama is very popular – and very beautiful. She wears the pearls," he chuckled.

As the subway thundered through the underground, I remembered the pearls: The depression had been in full swing. The cupboard had been bare and we were anxiously awaiting Papa's payday. Instead of giving the money to Mama, the church treasurer had given it directly to Papa. What a tragic mistake! Mama was the one to dole out street car tokens, and an occasional nickel for a cup of coffee, but Papa was noted for his liberal "giving freely all things." He had no concept of what feeding his family involved — nitty gritty scrimping and saving. Walking past a jewelry shop he saw a lovely string of pearls. At the same time, he felt the money in his pocket. Overjoyed at discovering his wealth, he purchased the pearls.

Bowing low, in great respect, he handed her the gift. "Mama, I suddenly realized I had never bought you a present. You have such a beautiful throat, you should wear pearls."

Mama never flinched. Tenderly she thanked him for the generous gift and promised to wear them always. She did! Later she told me, "There is a time and place for everything. Sometimes we need pearls more than potatoes. That was the time for pearls." Mama somehow saw that we survived until next payday.

"Next stop, Margaret." We emerged from the tunnel and walked past row houses, side by side, like children's blocks. Any plot of ground was neatly planted full of shrubs and flowers. On the front steps sat mothers and grandmothers keeping a watchful eye on all the neighborhood young, playing on the one-way streets.

Soon we were sitting in Mama's kitchen drinking coffee, laughing and talking — all at the same time. Starched lace curtains covered shining windows, and, in its proper place, stood the round mahogany table with the crystal vase. The upholstered furniture had been recovered, and a new carpet lay on the parlor floor. The dining room table was set for supper. Soon the family would be coming from school and work. Grace worked for the Y.M.C.A., earning thirty-five dollars a week. Doris and Gordon helped to carry the load with after-school jobs. Gordon had survived five sisters and a preacher-father, and had become one of the Brooklyn boys who played stickball in the streets. Joyce was cute, lovable, and sassy. She livened up her world with her own renditions of modern-day songs. Papa only heard her angelic voice – not the words of the songs. So if her voice were magic it seemed to make Papa blind to the lipstick, and deaf to her flirting phone calls that drove the boys wild. She even won a jitterbug contest. "Lilla Solveig" just had to sing for Papa "Flee as a bird to yon mountain," and his restless spirit quieted.

Jeanelle, the baby, was everyone's beloved. She was the joy of Mama's heart and the pride and delight of Papa's life, yet she managed to grow up unspoiled by it all. Years later she told me she once came home singing a popular tune, "A Little Bit Independent," and convinced Mama she had learned it in Sunday school.

Grace was Papa's church pianist, secretary, and confidante. She was his bridge over troubled family relationships. Grace set the pace in fashion and became a link between Mama's structured world and the cultural advantages of New York. Music was the common denominator in the family – just as long as it wasn't too "vorldly." Watching her so poised and self-assured I could hardly believe she was the mischievous sister who had gotten me into trouble as a child. It had been her idea to put soap on the kitchen floor, making it a skating rink or dance floor. That was fine — until I waltzed into Papa.

I was told how Barney miraculously walked in, out of the blue, during several stormy sessions. One such incident involved Papa discovering that Doris was in love with the Italian boy who worked at the local fruit market. Barney stepped in and kept Doris from running away from home. She had hidden under the porch, waiting for Papa's fury to subside. When she heard Barney's songs and laughter, she knew it was safe to "come home." It was good to know that Barney, with his Mildred, was still a part of our family: in Canada, in Chicago, and now in Brooklyn.

One by one, I watched the family gather around the table for supper, and, in unison, we asked the familiar Norwegian blessing. We eagerly passed the old bowls, full of meatballs and gravy and mashed potatoes, sculptured and decorated with parsley. The creamed cabbage, peas and carrots followed close behind. Lemon pie with whipped cream topped the dinner, and the endless cups of coffee completed the festive meal. Papa retreated to his study, while we children washed the dishes and chattered above the clatter. When we had put away the last dish and cleaned the sink until it sparkled, we all gathered in the parlor for music. Before retiring, we enjoyed a last cup of coffee and a quiet time of talk.

Mama was happy. God had allowed her to be close to Bestemor Bertilda, who lived in a small apartment within walking distance. Bestemor, who had known unbearable loneliness, was now surrounded by her children and grandchildren.

Some years later, on Easter Sunday, Bestemor sat down, folded her hands, and died. In quiet dignity, and dressed in her church-going best, she said a temporary "good night" to her precious children, Elvine and Joe, but a glorious "good morning" to her Lord — and Bernice. Jeanelle was the only one who overheard Mama sobbing out all her hurts and griefs when Bestemor died. Perhaps it was all the loneliness of her childhood that surfaced — but not for long. Mama washed her face, combed her hair, tied on a starched apron, and put on the coffee pot.

That Sunday morning we all walked to church. Papa, with reverent dignity, announced the opening hymn, "A Mighty Fortress Is Our God." Every head turned to nod to the pastor's daughter who was visiting from Chicago. There was a depth of understanding, compassion and mutual love that held these people together in an ever-increasing faith in God — and America. No one was allowed to be disrespectful to authority. They stood up for the National Anthem — even in the bathtub.

At the conclusion of the service I was welcomed into the family of Papa's church on Fifty-seventh Street.

During the week I was introduced to Brooklyn's Fifth Avenue, lined with small shops representing all the nationalities. I pushed Mama's cart to the fish market, where everyone spoke Norwegian. Each member of Mama's family and then each member of the proprietor's family had to be accounted for. The Danish bakery was fragrant with Danish pastry, and the displayed wedding cakes were a work of art. It was obvious that the Polish storekeeper kept up with the neighborhood children. We got Kosher dill pickles from a barrel in the Jewish delicatessen. The Italian fruit stand was a gathering place for everyone — especially the young.

"This is America, Margaret," exclaimed Mama, as if I didn't know. "No place in the world like this." Mama beamed, for she loved her international neighbors and stopped to visit along the way with all of them. "A little visit, Margaret, sometimes catches a problem before it is too late. Besides I learn whom to invite for coffee. A little talk with someone, and a little talk with God — it all helps to keep the wheels of the neighborhood running smoothly." Mama had her own way of curbing my impatience to get the shopping over with as soon as possible.

Weddings, births, music lessons, and report cards were duly reported along the way. Such topics make conversation flow in any language. The immigrants shared a mutual interest in each other's children, the first generation of Americans.

Over coffee cups I heard stories from Norway. From Mama's girlhood friends, whom I had never met before, I heard old tales about their fears of the unknown land, their dreams for their children, and their struggle to learn the new language. I sensed the treasure of friendships, deeply rooted in mutual respect and need, but matured with the sun and rain of joy and sorrow. The tapestry of lifelong friendships was made with the perfect blend of brightly-colored threads and pastel shades of patience and thankfulness.

Before returning to Chicago, I took one last ride on the Staten Island ferry. Across dark waters I saw the Lady With the Lamp looking out over the harbor. A lonely fog horn woke the lure of the sea that had slept deep within me. In my heart I crossed the Atlantic to the fjords and cliffs I had never seen. Someday I would. Wrapping my coat around me I wondered how the fifteen-year-old Elvine felt when the ocean liner eased into the embrace of the Lady With the Lamp.

I was about to venture into my own new world. My trip would not take me across the ocean, but down the aisle of Papa's church to take my place beside Harold who would there, in front of all these Brooklyn witnesses, become my husband.

I yearned to complete my journey as well as Mama had hers — both her journey in the new land and her journey beside Papa. I trusted she had taught me well.

And so it came to pass that I married Harold in Papa's church on June 30, 1938. Gordon and all my dear sisters stood with me, facing Papa and hearing his solemn words.

After our honeymoon trip to Cooperstown, New York, Niagara Falls, and down through Canada, we returned to Chicago where we began our new life together. I continued nursing while Harold completed his graduate degree at Northern Baptist Theological Seminary.

fifteen

Love It Back to Life, Mother

"STANDING ON THE PROMISES, watching all the girls go by."

The five-year-old singer stood in the reception hall, feet firmly planted and arms folded across his starched white shirt and bow tie. His polished shoes shone on the soft carpet, and his blond hair, parted on one side, was slick and trim. He sang with all the confidence of a seasoned performer, and enjoyed the applause of his amused audience – the guests attending the annual open house. This was his first day in the Norwegian Children's Home, Brooklyn, New York.

Mama, unaware of the "one man show" in the reception hall, was giving her full attention to the last minute details of hosting the children's home open house.

Enjoying a brief visit to New York, I followed Mama around and was utterly amazed at her ability to attend to innumerable details, when she was continually interrupted to answer a child's question or to make an important decision. She flowed through the days like a river, bringing refreshment to many a dry bank. She reminded me of the man described in Psalm 1, who was "a tree planted by the rivers of water."

Mama had received a call. "The board of directors asked me to be the superintendent of the children's home, a place for homeless Norwegian children. The parents of some are very ill. Others are missing or dead. The children from a family are kept together, so, here I am, a mother again."

The wise men behind the scenes saw the compassionate heart of a universal mother, and an ability to discipline and motivate others in love. God saw an obedient child, walking out her loving faith in Him who could do anything, who would never fail her.

So, Mama accepted the call to become the superintendent of the Norwegian Children's Home. Papa served as chaplain and social worker. They relinquished the pastorate at the First Norwegian Baptist Church, to serve together in the children's home, but the fellowship and worship in their local church continued.

Today was open house. The warm sunlight cast a glow over the neatly-trimmed gardens. Every room in the beautiful brick house was in order. The children had been rehearsing songs and readings, and, of course, proper manners. Bright hairbows and matching socks complemented polished shoes, ruffles and lace. The boys stood like starched penguins, in dark suits and white shirts. Every hair rested in place. Only mischievous eyes refused conformity.

Johnny, the new boy, had arrived in time to be scrubbed, combed and outfitted in a new suit. He had been told that visitors were coming to see him. He was to stand still and watch. He stood still, but couldn't resist putting on a show.

Within moments of his rendition of standing and watching, he was gathered into perfumed arms and smothered with kisses. When an older boy led him away, Johnny waved happily to all the new-found friends who had come to see him.

Yesterday he had been alone. His mother had been taken to King's County Hospital, and no one could find his father. A distant relative brought him to the "home," where he discovered a new family life.

The ruffled girls swished alongside their guests and excitedly showed them their treasures — quilts they had made for their beds and stuffed animals that kept a silent watch over the neat dormitory. Mama insisted that each child have a box of his or her own in which to store personal treasures. I overheard one girl: "I never had a treasure box before, and no one can peek. I made my quilt. Debbie is five. She is my little sister and I take care of her. I help her dress and lay out her clothes for kindergarten. I braid her pigtails and match her socks and ribbons. I taught her to tie her laces and the bow on her dress. Each one has a brother or sister. Like a family, you know. Some have visitors, but I have no one. Will you be my visitor?"

The older woman, plump and silver-haired, squeezed the girl's hand and, in her soft Norwegian accent, promised to be her visitor. She opened her purse and pulled out a perfumed handkerchief, "Karen, put this in your treasure box, and next time I'll bring you a picture. Perhaps we can take a picture of you, for me to keep." That was the beginning of a long friendship.

"Young man, I understand you'll soon be eighteen and leaving the home."

"Yes, sir, but I don't know where to go," Tom answered the distinguished white-haired executive he was escorting on the tour of the boy's dormitory.

"I'll be your friend and help you get to college, or find a job. Here's my card, just call me anytime. We can always find time to talk things over. By the way, what happened to you, young man? The last time I was here you were skipping out at night and having problems at school. In fact, several of you boys were about to be sent to correctional school. What happened?"

"Mother Tweten, that's what happened.

"I'll never forget the first night she came to our dormitory. We had planned some bold adventures and waited for her to make her rounds. Instead, she sat down on Bob's bed, sang Norwegian songs and read the Bible and prayed for each one of us by name. She got up and kissed us all good night and told us she loved us. When she left she stood by the door and said, 'God bless you, *my* boys.' We couldn't carry out our plans. The next night she sat on Ted's bed, told a story, read, sang, and prayed. She kissed us good night and said 'God bless you, *my* boys.'

"Then one night she came in and sat on the wrong bed. Bill jumped up and said, 'You sat on Ted's bed twice. It's my turn tonight.' None of us went to reform school. The tough guy, Bill, got saved at the Billy

Graham Crusade in Madison Square Garden. The next night he made Bob go forward, 'Get saved or I'll beat you up!' he said."

Downstairs in the dining room an air of festivity reigned. The older boys cared for the younger and the guests were served by happy children. Church groups and women's clubs mingled with dignitaries from government and businessmen, and with news reporters. The children sensed their importance and rose with honor to the occasion. This was a special day; Mama had made them a part of the festivities.

No one had believed that forty to fifty children could be beautifully disciplined in gracious courtesy. But they didn't know Mama! Papa, handsome as ever, enjoyed the guests and with great flourish practiced all his old Norwegian jokes. The businessmen who had founded the home looked at their fulfilled dream. Mama saw the thread of love that had been interwoven between frightened children and these adults − lonely immigrants who had persevered at building schools, hospitals, even the children's home. Mama was proud of her children. When they performed before their enthusiastic audience, a sense of worth crept into their once frightened, empty hearts. They basked in the love and approval of their mother and felt safe within the walls of their home.

To conclude the day's program, Mama told the story of the dead plant.

"One day Susie came in from the playground, holding a broken pot with a wilted plant in her muddy hands.

"She begged me, 'Please don't throw away the plant.'

"'But Susie, the plant is dead,' I said.

"'Then you must love it back to life, Mother.'

"She thrust the wilted plant into my hand and skipped away, completely confident that its life would return. I placed the remains of this plant in a new flower pot filled with fresh dirt. The sun filtered through the Brooklyn skies and warmed the lifeless plant that sat on my windowsill. Every day I watered my little wilted garden and waited. One day a green shoot appeared, and now a lovely green plant thrives on my sill.

"When someone brings us a frightened, wilted, hurt child, I hear my Susie say, 'Love it back to life, Mother!' So many human relationships can be loved back to life. For me the most rewarding are those with a child, who has been wilted and abandoned in a broken flower pot or home. For a child who then is thrust into my hand, 'Love him back to life' is my highest command. You people of Norway gave me a flower pot, this lovely home, and God pours His love through us — to love them back to life.

"I thank you."

The sun set over the gardens and brick walls. The children were tucked in their beds. The steps of the guests had echoed down the walk. The door had closed behind them. Mama sat down to a quiet cup of coffee. The amber glow of love had wrapped a warm blanket over the weak and strong together. She opened her Bible and read, "Inasmuch as ye have done it unto one of the least of these My brethren, ye have done it unto me" (Matthew 25:40).

sixteen

Someone to Come Home To

MAMA CLOSED THE DOOR to her office and slumped to her knees in utter exhaustion. "I can't go on! I can't!" She wept into her folded arms, "My strength is gone! I cry to Thee, oh Lord, for Thou alone are my strong tower. Even Moses cried to You when the task was too great. You said, 'Moses, there is a place by Me, in the cleft of the rock, until the storm passes by.' I know You are Creator of heaven and earth – a God of miracles. Today I ask one special thing, please send me a cook."

Homesick for her beloved land, the cook had left suddenly for Norway. In addition to all the administrative duties, Mama had to fill the void in the kitchen, cooking for forty-five children.

Days, months, and years were speeding out of control, like a train that wouldn't stop. She tried to get off some place, to acclimate herself to life on solid ground but the train moved faster.

She arose quietly and opened her Bible, "They that wait upon the LORD shall renew their strength; they shall mount up with wings as eagles; they shall run, and not be weary; and they shall walk and not faint" (Isa. 40:31). "Come unto Me, all ye that labor and are heavy laden, and I will give you rest" (Matt. 11:28).

As she did every day, Mama spoke to the silent pictures of her own children. All but Jeanelle had flown Mama's nest; Mama prayed for us across the miles. "Oh, my children, God is your refuge. He never fails." Turning the pages of her Bible, she read again, "I will never leave thee, nor forsake thee," and "I can do all things through Christ which strengtheneth me."

Quietly, softly, the Word became a living sound. By rote Mama repeated verses that floated randomly through her mind. "The LORD is my light and my salvation." "God is my refuge and strength." "Casting all your care upon Him for He careth for you."

The quiet was broken by an insistent knock at the door. "There is someone to see you, Mrs. Tweten."

Pausing for a moment, Mama breathed in the strength that God had renewed in her. She allowed the mantle of love to cover her with the "peace that passeth understanding." She closed her Bible and went to the door to greet her visitor.

Before her stood a plump Norwegian woman. In broken English she said, "I don't speak much English, but I need vork. Could you use a cook?"

"Before they call, I will answer," came to Mama's mind.

A few days later a distraught mother with six children came to Mama's waiting room. "Please take my children!" she pleaded. Huddled in silent fear, the children clung to their mother's skirt. "I can't go on! My strength is gone and I can't manage another day!"

"Come, let's have a cup of coffee, and we can talk," comforted Mama. The children ate cookies apprehensively and watched quietly. "I recently said those same words," continued Mama, "but God gave me an answer. Let me read it to you. We'll pray together and ask God for a miracle. In the meantime, just hold on for one week. Keep your children with you. They need you. Trust Him for a miracle, and see what happens."

"Yes, I'll try a little longer," she answered. She gathered her children and returned home.

Weeks passed before Mama remembered the distraught woman and decided to visit her. When she saw the abandoned rat-infested basement flat she had sent the woman back to, she wept. No wonder the woman had given up — or had she? Where could she have gone?

An elderly man, leaning on a cane, called to Mama, "Hey lady, they ain't here no more. She was going to put her kids in an orphanage and then she decided to try one more week. You know something? The old man got a real good job in Chicago and came for her and the kids. He had a nice clean flat — an upstairs flat with steam heat — waiting for them. It happened so fast, lady. In a week they were gone."

"Oh, thank you, sir, and God bless you. I'll come back to visit you." Mama remembered, "Who comforteth us in all our tribulation, that we may be able to comfort them which are in any trouble, by the com-

fort wherewith we ourselves are comforted of God"
(2 Corinthians 1:4).

Returning to the children's home, Mama opened
the door humming softly one of her favorite songs,
"Be not dismayed whate'er betide; God will take care
of you."

The nurse met Mama at the door. "Bobby is sick."

"Not Bobby!"

Impulsively, Mama picked a flower from the patch
by the porch and took it to Bobby. His fever was high
and he breathed heavily. Within moments Dr. Fanta
was on his way and four-year-old Bobby was taken to
Lutheran Deaconess Hospital. In his hands he
clutched the wilting flower.

Mama went with him, but she couldn't stay away
from the home all day.

"I'll be back, Bobby. I have work to do, but I'll
be back to see you later. Just hold the flower and let
it remind you that I'll be back." With these words
Mama left to attend to administrative duties. In the
meantime the nurses talked amongst themselves, "Too
bad, his mother is dead," commented one. "He has no
one, you know."

Half asleep Bobby overhead the words that
floated through the door, "His mother is dead, He has
no one." He drifted into a semi-coma, and some time
passed before he was fully conscious again. Suddenly
he sat up. The first thing he saw was Mama holding
fresh flowers.

"You're not dead! You're not dead!"

"No Bobby. Of course I'm not dead. Of course I
am your mother. You'll always belong to me, no mat-

ter how old you get."

He fell asleep, clutching a fresh flower, and Mama sat beside him, praying and singing.

"Everyone needs to belong to someone," Mama thought. "God says we belong to Him. He bought us with His Son."

One day when the "big boys," fourteen- to sixteen-year-olds, were helping in the kitchen, Mama overheard their conversation: "When we become eighteen we have to leave the home," one boy said.

Another commented, "I'm going into the service."

A third boy said, "I'm going to college."

The fourth boy was quiet.

"What are you thinking about?" Mama asked Tommy.

"Mother, whom do we come home to when we go away?"

"Boys, you can come home to me!"

"Will you always be here?"

"You can come home, wherever I am."

The boys finished their chores. With an impulsive hug, Tommy reassured himself, "We have to have someone to come home to."

Mama remembered Psalm 90:1: "God is our dwelling place [our Home] in all generations."

We all have Someone to come home to.

seventeen

St. Olav's Medal

IT WAS A BEAUTIFUL NOVEMBER DAY in Georgia. Red and gold leaves outside my kitchen window looked like a patchwork quilt. Kennesaw Mountain loomed in the distance, a sentinel against the blue sky. "Tomorrow," I thought, "I will rake the leaves, but now I will enjoy a cup of coffee and look over the morning mail. There it was — a letter from Mama, in her own characteristic handwriting (which we had, over the years, learned to interpret).

Sunday, November 16, 1951

Dear Margaret, Harold, and children,

Thank you for your letter, and I am glad all is well.

Tonight I have extra news! I was decorated last night with the St. Olav's Medal from King Haaken of Norway.

We had our annual banquet — set for two hundred people, with outstanding speakers and a fine program. The Norwegian consul, who has been our guest speaker for the last five years, was here last night. At the close of his speech he asked me to come for-

ward. Then he spoke of the work I had done at the
home, and recommended that I get the St. Olav's
Medal. (The king had been told of my work.) He
pinned the medal on me and gave me a diploma with
the king's seal and signature. All the people stood.
I just could not talk, but I had to say something, so
I said, "I only wish my six children were here. I do
not deserve it, but I take it. Grace and love from
God." The photographer was there and pictures will
be in the Nordisk Tidende (Norwegian Times). I will
send you the paper. Fortunately, I had on a beautiful
black velvet dress, made to order for the banquet.

When I was in the hospital last year, the president
of the children's home came to see me and we had a
long visit. He asked about the family, past and present — where we had lived, what churches we had
pastored, and where all you children are now.

I suppose the record is with the king. Something
for the children and grandchildren to remember. You
know this is next to the highest honor given by the
Norwegian government. I still can't believe it. I
wonder what dad will think, when he hears. It is
already in the papers in Norway. If I lived there, I
would have to go to the king and thank him person-
ally, but here I will do it through the consul. Well, I
thank the Lord for it all. I know I now have a greater
responsibility and I need the Lord all the more. Don't
forget to pray for me.

I wore the new velvet dress and medal to church
this morning.

Doris, Gordon, and families are coming for
Thanksgiving.

With love to all of you,

Your loving mother

My coffee was cold, but warm tears fell in my lap
— tears of gratitude for the honor Mama so richly

deserved and tears for all of us who hadn't been there to rejoice with her.

I knew no photographer could have caught the wistfulness of Mama saying, "I wish my children were here." I thought about "the children" — Grace, working in New York, Gordon, married and teaching in New York. Doris was graduated from Wheaton College and married to David Hammer. Joyce Solveig was married to Harold's brother, Howard. Jeanelle, the baby, was studying at Columbia Bible College.

I found myself back in the Norwegian diary reliving the fright of a fifteen-year-old immigrant girl, determined to find her mother. I saw her as the faithful servant in a Jewish home, using her leisure hours to probe libraries. I was back on the Canadian prairie, listening to the promise: "The bluebirds will come; just wait and see." Humility and dignity walked with her as the garment of praise covered her. "Always keep a thankful heart, Margaret." My mind's image of the coffee pot sitting on the cookstove reminded me to refill my cup and look ahead. Mama would go to see the king. Of that I was sure!

I was also sure that when the day came for her to stand before the King of Kings, she would proudly say, "I am glad my children are here."

Three years later, in July 1954, Mama boarded the Stavangerfjord and visited her beloved Norway. She traveled with Papa, visiting his homestead, their relatives, and friends. They kept his speaking engagements. She saw the country, the cities, even the palace and the king, with whom she had a fifteen-minute audience to thank him for the medal. What a thrill that was for her. He made her feel as though she were sitting in her own parlor and talking to a good friend.

She and Papa saw the church of Norway first-hand, and rejoiced in God's work among His people.

The letters winged back and forth to us children. When I read the reports of her activities, I marveled at her endurance, and wondered at the grace of God, who chooses His vessels, not always the great and powerful, but even this small, humble, obedient, faithful child of His.

She came home in September, returning to her forty needy charges. But we, her six children and twelve grandchildren, had missed her as much as those who lived in the children's home.

She settled back into her mothering duties and God continued to bless her faithfulness. Early in 1959 she sent me a copy of the children's home annual report, showing God's presence.

Annual Report To
The Norwegian Children's Home Association
January 20, 1959

"They that trust in the LORD shall be as mount Zion, which cannot be removed, but abideth for ever. As the mountains are round about Jerusalem, so the LORD is round about his people from henceforth even for ever" (Psalm 125:1-2).

It has been a blessing all through the year to know and realize this truth, that as mountains are round about Jerusalem, so the Lord is round about His people. We have felt it as a large family. The Lord has been round about us. He has protected us from sickness and sorrow. He has guided us through our problems and has supplied all of our needs and blessed us with His own presence.

We started the year with thirty-six children. Ten have been admitted and eleven discharged, so that at the end of the year we had thirty-five children, twenty-two boys and thirteen girls.

Some time ago, I was telling the Christmas story to the nursery group how the shepherds were out on the field taking care of the sheep and the lambs, and how the angel came from heaven with the good news that the Baby Jesus was born — a Savior was born — and the whole choir of angels came and sang, "Glory to God in the highest." When all the angels went back to heaven, the shepherds said, "Come on, let us go to Bethlehem and see this thing — let us go and find the Baby Jesus," and so they went to Bethlehem to find Jesus.

One little boy spoke up and said, "Who took care of the sheep, while the shepherds went away?" Well in all my days, I had never thought of that before. Just who did take care of the sheep while the shepherds went away? You have to answer a child, and I think I said something like, "God would take care of them." Anyway, the child was satisfied, but later I started thinking. Who takes care of our homes and our children while we go about our duties? We send thirty children to school every morning. They go to five different schools, in five different directions, so it would be impossible for me to follow them and watch over them. Who takes care of them? God.

I pray every morning, "God bless the children as they go to school; watch over those at home." The Lord is round about His people, and we humbly bow in thanksgiving and praise.

As I continued reading the ten-page report, I was amazed at the variety of cultural and stimulating activities scheduled for each month.

The report concluded with:

> We fixed up a party for New Year's Eve, and as the hours grew late, we sat around the table and read part of Psalm 92, then thanked the Lord for His faithfulness and many blessings. "It is a good thing to give thanks unto the LORD, and to sing praises unto Thy name O, most High: to show forth Thy loving-kindness in the morning, and Thy faithfulness every night."
>
> Thus we entered prayerfully into the new year of 1959.

"For everything there is a season." The days and months added up to seventeen years of loving service at the Norwegian Children's Home. But now it was time to softly close that door and reopen another. Papa returned to his first love, the pulpit of the church on Fifty-seventh Street. Together they walked through the old door, a little slower, but in step with God's plan for the years ahead.

King Haakon could be proud of his people. One day his son Olav, the new king of Norway, would visit the Norwegian Children's Home in Brooklyn and pay tribute to the hard work and warm hearts of those people. They came to America, not only to be blessed, but to give back blessings with good measure and running over.

eighteen

The Golden Wedding

THE FIRST NORWEGIAN BAPTIST CHURCH on Fifty-
seventh Street in Brooklyn, New York, was ablaze with
light. It was June 18, 1965. People came from every
direction to attend the golden wedding anniversary
celebration for Pastor and Mrs. E. N. Tweten. The
Polish storekeeper, the Italian fruit stand owner, the
Jewish merchant, all a part of the "Oslo Boulevard"
(Brooklyn's Eighth Avenue), closed their shops early
to join their neighbors: the owners of the fish market,
the delicatessen, the gift shop, and Christiansen's
Bakery. Mingling accents from the old world joined
the Scandinavians in the happy occasion meant for
all of them.

Tonight Mama's children and grandchildren
would pay their tribute of love, by doing what Papa
told the world his children could do — sing and play
music. With Grace and Jeanelle at the organ and
piano, Gordon directed the rehearsals. There was no
doubt about it. Mama's children would sing. With her
usual efficiency, Grace coordinated the festivities.

The music poured forth as visiting dignitaries joined members and friends in the pews of Papa's church. A pause — then the majestic wedding march brought every person to his feet. Mama in her golden dress came down the aisle on Papa's arm. Behind them marched friends who had attended their wedding fifty years before. Uncle Joseph Johnson, Nick Olsen, Ida Breding, Olga Bjornsen, Marie Anderson, Fred and Oline Johnson, Aslak and Ingeborg Halvorsen.

Songs from the grandchildren brought smiles of approval. Tears came to many when Mama's children and their families sang "God Leads His Dear Children Along."

When we sang in Norwegian "He the Pearly Gates Will Open," everyone smiled and nodded approval, especially Mama.

Gordon presented Mama and Papa with a large picture of us children and our families.

Papa, white hair glistening, looked at his old friends and chuckled, "Ya, there is only one Mama!" Mama's soft gray hair framed her glowing face, "Papa, in spite of all your faults, you have been a faithful lover." That brought down the house and paved the way for the reception that followed.

Hot coffee was poured into countless cups as guests came to the beautiful table laden with international delicacies. In the center was a large Danish layer cake, with fresh strawberries and whipped cream.

Visiting among the guests, and shaking hands with everyone, was the state senator, who was a frequent guest at these celebrations. He brought his coffee cup over and joined me for a brief visit. With a sweep of his hand, he looked over the crowd: "This is

America, and I love it! This is where I get my faith in people renewed. Margaret, you must write it down, all the stories and traditions. We all need to be reminded of our heritage, and what makes America!"

During the reception Mama disappeared for a few moments. She returned wearing her original wedding dress. An Italian photographer, standing close to me, exclaimed, "My God, she is simply beautiful!" Tears fell on his cheeks as he snapped pictures. Mama, whose silver hair looked like a halo and whose blue eyes brimmed with happiness, stood in her lace dress and posed for her wedding picture. Fifty years ago there had been no picture. Papa bought books instead. Tonight she had her wedding picture.

Now it was my turn to gather the memories of the past.

Fifty Golden Years

They walk in beauty from the night
To golden sunrise,
Not the sundown.
Ahead the glory of Eternal Light,
The welcome skies
And jeweled crown.

Two hearts were born from fjords and cliffs,
The midnight sun
And snow-filled dale.
Across the foamy ocean crest
A new world begun,
By God's grace blessed.

Two lives were blended into one
To give the glow
Of human touch.
Not counting cost — His will be done;
The world must know

God gave so much.

Youth with courage born of surrender,
Strength from submission
To lose, not gain,
Wove golden cords of love made tender,
Earth's highest mission,
Giving life again.

Canadian blizzards and wind-swept field,
Midnight's lone hour,
The heat of day:
Outstretched hands, humble hearts to yield
To God's power
Life — Truth — The Way.

Cold hands warmed by the open hearth,
A rocking chair
And coffee cup.
Heavy hearts turned to God's love and new birth,
A humble prayer
And a welcome sup.

The children grew with sense of belonging
To the Master's Plan,
Children of God.
To trust, obey, and serve without yearning
Ambitions to scan,
Worldly fame to plod.

Memories come with haunting remembering
Of humble fare,
A warm loaf of bread.
With love, mirth, and time for singing,
A table to share,
White linen spread.

Dad preached with fervor God's matchless grace
On wind-swept plain,
Pulpit or mission.
Mother saw the searching, lonely face,

The hidden pain
Or lost ambition.

Together they gave, no thought of gaining,
Love to a child,
Hope to mankind.
They took human driftwood without blaming
Those sin had beguiled.
Or darkness made blind.

The old hymns echo through turbulent years
Of war and plunder;
Depression's hour.
God's promises stood — faith dispels fears.
Men's schemes torn asunder
By God's mighty power.

For fifty years two hearts bent tender
To give, not gain;
To lose, not win.
For greatness comes in complete surrender
In service, not fame,
God's peace within.

They walk in beauty from the night
To glorious sunrise,
Not the sundown.
Ahead the glow of eternal Light,
Golden skies,
The Father's home.

nineteen

Bless This House

"To EVERYTHING THERE IS A SEASON." The "call" had come full cycle, for here, in Brooklyn, New York, the bride and groom had begun their ministry. Now at the age of 82, Papa was closing the door. He had been preaching God's Word for 67 years.

One by one we brought our families and sàt in the familiar pews of Papa's church. We heard again the old Norwegian songs and listened to Papa expound from his open Bible to his faithful congregation. Some had been part of Mama and Papa's wedding many years ago. All were one loving family who rejoiced and wept together, who knew each other's weaknesses and strengths, but who had learned to love and forgive.

When the church family stood to sing "God Be With You Till We Meet Again," many knew that the next meeting would be "at Jesus' feet." Papa raised his hands to pronounce the familiar benediction:

Now unto him that is able to keep you from falling, and to present you faultless before the presence of His glory with exceeding joy, To the only wise God our

Savior, be glory and majesty, dominion and power, both now and ever. Amen" (Jude 24,25).

While we helped to pack dishes and dismantle Papa's study, we saw Papa's white anguish; he was taking down his beloved books from their familiar shelves. By midnight the shelves were empty.

"Come, Papa, now we have coffee." We sat and talked of the goodness of God and the impending move to Florida, where Mama and Papa would be near Jeanelle, their "baby." At last we said good night, but Papa didn't follow our lead and go to bed. He sat quietly and read his Bible. In the morning we noticed Papa's face. It had aged overnight. When we went into the study, we saw that he had returned the books to their shelves.

When our brother, Gordon, saw the anguish, he stepped in, "I'll take care of the books and send them to you when you have room."

"Ya, that is good, Gordon." Papa sat in his study, oblivious to all the commotion around him. God and Mama would have to tend to the packing. He had to linger with his familiar friends on the bookshelves.

Plantation, Florida

My dear Margaret,

Many thanks for your lovely letter. I just want you to know we are so very happy in our new home. I just thank the Lord all day, while we are fussing and fixing, getting everything ready. Jeanelle and Joel have been wonderful. Tonight Jeanelle is coming to take Dad and me to buy some "Florida" clothes. He is feeling fine, and just enjoys his books and a beautiful color TV that Grace gave us. We even have our phone in. Grace saw to that. She is wonderful, and works too hard for us.

I have a darling kitchen, a dining room, large parlor, two good-sized bedrooms, linen closet, and a nice front porch with grass and flowers all around.

Your loving mother

In the meantime, Doris and David Hammer had built their Williamsburg dream home on their land in Stoneville, North Carolina. Across the mountains and valleys the wind blew through the pines. "So much like Norway," Papa mused when he saw it. We later realized that Mama had been happier in Florida than he had. How much he wanted to go to North Carolina, although he was learning to be content with what he had and where he was. He wrote the following letter, which I cherish, as he wrote so seldom.

Plantation, Florida
December 17, 1972

Dear Margaret,

So you want a letter from your father, and will frame it, hang it on the wall so everybody can see it, and read it. Isn't that something?

What can a father possibly say to be worthy of such honor?

Mother is extremely happy here and feels fine and looks radiant. I miss Brooklyn. This is a desert place, no buses, no ferries, no subways. I keep singing "Don't fence me in."

God be with you and your family, as He has in the past. You just continue to live in the shadow of the Almighty, sheltered by the God who is above all gods. That all things will go well with you and yours.

With much love, Father

The Hammers decided to build a small dream house across the road for Mama and Papa. With joy and pride Mama and Papa insisted on making a small financial investment toward the building costs. Mama would have her own home at last, the first since the four-room yellow house on Avenue J in Canada. Papa would have his own study, for his beloved books. They waited contentedly in Florida for the house to be completed.

They came to Stoneville in March 1973. Papa came, not to live in his dream house, but to be buried, just below it in the family cemetery.

When Papa was 85, God quietly ushered him into the presence of the King of Kings. Jeanelle's home church in Fort Lauderdale honored Papa with a memorial service, not as a stranger in their midst, but as a faithful servant of God, one with them. Then he came to North Carolina.

Now Mama and her children stood by the gray casket, while the March wind blew through the pines.

The old Scandinavian names from Chicago and Brooklyn were, in the main, missing, but new friends, with American names surrounded Mama with the same love.

My husband, Harold, conducted the graveside memorial service. He quoted Papa's favorite psalms, the twenty-third and the ninetieth: "'Lord, Thou hast been our dwelling place in all generations. From everlasting to everlasting, Thou art God.'

"Here was a man in whom there was no guile. A man who never doubted God, but stood up for Jesus and believed in and defended the Bible as God's divinely inspired Word. Of him we could honestly say, 'Blessed are the pure in heart: for they shall see God.' "

Harold concluded the service with Papa's familiar benediction:

Now the God of peace, that brought again from the dead our Lord Jesus, that great shepherd of the sheep, through the blood of the everlasting covenant, Make you perfect in every good work to do His will, working in you that which is well-pleasing in His sight, through Jesus Christ; to whom be glory for ever and ever. Amen (Hebrews 13:20-21).

We couldn't grieve, for somehow, in our imagination, we saw him in the libraries of heaven, talking with his beloved authors, Charles Haddon Spurgeon and Matthew Henry. From out of the past came the lawgiver Moses, the prophet Isaiah, the poet David, philosophers, teachers, and preachers. The living Book was now alive to Papa. He left his books to meet the authors, particularly the Author and Finisher of his faith.

And so it came to pass that Mama came alone to her dream home. The new friends with the American names stood in the golden sunlight and sang:

Bless this house Oh Lord we pray
Keep it safe by night and day.

Mama, holding David Hammer's arm, walked across the road to open the door to her own dream home.

They came again, the young and the old, the lonely ones, the friends. They found the coffee pot hot and heard stories of love and faith. The First Baptist Church of Stoneville, North Carolina, became Mama's home church, and the Reverend Mr. Ward Burch her friend and pastor.

She became a symbol of strength to senior citizens and a source of wisdom to the young. At the festive occasions she shared her readings and stories. Most of all she loved the family weddings, when she walked down the aisle on the arm of one of her handsome grandsons, to be seated in a place of honor. Her face was wreathed in smiles. Always displaying a new dress and orchid, she greeted guests at the receptions, whispering her own special blessing to her grandchildren. The beautiful brides smiled, "Grandmother, you stole the show." How she loved them all. God blessed her and all who entered her yellow dream house.

Mama's quiet faith never wavered, but her steps grew feeble. Not quite three years later, in December 1975 I brought her to live in our home in Greensboro, North Carolina, thirty-five miles from Stoneville. Since Grace lived nearby she drove Mama to her church in Stoneville when Mama was able to attend. Dr. James Bruce came often to have a cup of tea and keep a watchful eye on Mama.

She walked softly among us and our house was blessed.

twenty

The Sweater

TULIPS, LIKE TOY SOLDIERS, stood in a row. Pansies laughed into the sunshine. It was spring and Dr. Bruce gave Mama permission to return to her own home for a birthday visit. Joyce flew in from Chicago to help, and, in her thoughtful way, tended to little things the rest of us failed to notice. She repotted Mama's violets into brightly-colored flower pots. She mended and sorted clothes for the summer months ahead.

Jeanelle, who had flown up from Florida, helped Mama sort out her thoughts and ideas as to how to give away her small treasures. They decided to paste names on the different items, so each one in the family would receive a small token of her thoughtfulness. Her real treasures were laid up in heaven. This we all knew, but her careful marking of a vase, a pitcher, or a special plate made us all aware of her quiet orderly way of living.

Mama also knew that this time when she would leave, and close the door to her dream home, she would not return again. So she set her heart on preparing for the journey to her heavenly home. The day was warm and sunny, and Mama was once again in her own kitchen. Before setting her hands to the task ahead, she announced, "First we have coffee."

When the evening sun dipped behind the mountains, Mama and her children gathered around the festive table in Doris's big house. Mama received her cake and candles, gifts and greetings with delighted joy. One gift, however, brought Mama's glasses down on her nose. Peering at the gift-wrapped cane, she paused. I explained hastily that it was to keep Duke and Duchess from tripping her on her walks to the mail box. The dogs would have sniffed at that lame excuse, for they walked sedately beside her until she sat down in the rocker to read her mail. There they stretched out, with ears at attention, while she read the mail out loud. Then she folded the letters in neat packets and rocked gently. She was remembering and praying for each writer.

As she did with all her mail, she would read this year's birthday greetings again, and place them in neat packets. Each gift was an expression of love, especially the guitar. The days of the string band came back with plaintive memories while Mama strummed the familiar chords and sang the old songs. I couldn't help but remember when Papa played the guitar in my kitchen in Georgia, and sang a Norwegian love song he had written for Mama when he was in Norway. "What did Mama say when she first heard it?" I asked. Papa answered softly, "She didn't say anything, she just cried."

I wished I had written down Papa's love song to Mama.

After the dinner and gifts, we went into the den, where the best gifts of all were the joy of laughter and remembering that the sun and rain of life work together for good. We had learned through the years that laughter cushions life's hurts and keeps them from becoming embittered scars.

Tonight we missed Gordon, our brother. The wind sighed over his grave, next to Papa's, just below the hill. In June 1975, God had taken Gordon, Mama's only son, home. Home to heaven, home to North Carolina. He had been only 52, in our eyes not old enough to leave us, but who knows the ways of God?

In his earlier days cynicism had dogged Gordon's steps. He had been consumed with his work, intellectualism, and the challenges of chess, yet the reality of faith had lingered on the back roads of his mind. He had Alice, his adored wife, and Ray, Nancy, Don, and Kurt – his children. Out of a sense of duty he attended Papa's Brooklyn church. Throughout most of his life Papa couldn't understand his son's true worth.

Through a personal encounter with the love of God, Gordon turned from the restless river. He saw that vague, intellectual theology wasn't enough, that Jesus and His power were real. From his innermost being flowed rivers of living water that refreshed the dry banks around him. With a compassionate touch he reached into broken lives. He and Alice (a warm hearth, complete with slippers for tired feet) opened their home to the restless searching ones.

Gordon and Grace stimulated each other with their mutual love of books and music, with their romance with the city of New York. Doris shared her adventures in faith with Gordon's warm, responsive heart. He had closed no doors to his five sisters. Father, lost in his theology, couldn't hear his children, but his son had been blessed with Mama's gift of compassionate listening.

Then God took him. In the hospital room Doris sensed his spirit winging homeward. Alice walked the lonely hospital hall. Just as her soul reached its midnight hour, a song burst forth: "Because He lives, I can face tomorrow."

At the memorial service for Gordon, Jewish, Catholic, and Protestant friends joined in a hymn of praise to God. They had seen a man walk with God on earth, and now, in perfect understanding, Papa and his son walked with God in heaven.

Surely goodness and mercy shall follow me all the days of my life: and I will dwell in the house of the LORD for ever (Ps. 23:6).

Just as memories can break and burn, so memories can bind and bless. With remembering came the tears that washed our eyes so that we could see the plan of God over a lifetime, a plan that is bigger than what we see if we look at individual days.

Gordon Lund Tweten

June 15, 1975

The sound of taps across the hill,
　A silent pause,
And the world was still.
A swaying branch of scented pine,
　Gentle breezes
Over the hills of time.

She walked away from thudding sound,
    The wilted flowers
Brown, newly turned ground.
A soft caress on gold-spun hair,
    Years turned back,
Her child was there.

"My son, my son, my only son" –
    A skyward glance
Asked why – he was too young
To leave behind the ones
    Who need him so.
Her faltering steps were slow.

Friends, loved ones moved in tread
    Across the grass,
Where loving hands a table spread.
Remembering earth's sorrows pass;
    From God all blessings flow;
Praise Him all creatures here below.

Night comes like shadows o'er the hill;
    The North Star shines.
She walks alone while all is still
And whispers softly – "He was mine.
    We walked life's way
As one – now – and forever."

"He came alone to touch the earth
    Wet with tears.
He was my dad, eternal worth
For my young years. I miss his step
    Outside the door,
His understanding love much more."

"We also came who loved him so,
    Five of us as one,
Why did this dear one have to go
Husband, father, friend, and son.

We stood, one with the other,
To us he was our only brother."

"I, too, came in the early dawn,
    Took his hand.
For we had walked the city streets
And healed the hurts of sin's defeats
    Come away, My own
In heavenly places take your stand.

"He walked so close to Me on earth,
    Heard My voice.
Counted this world of little worth,
His hands were lifted to rejoice,
    To worship and adore
I whispered, 'Friend, come Home, forevermore.'

"He turned to give one fleeting look
    To reach your hand
I said, 'Trust Me — they are in My Book;
Together you will someday stand.'
    He turned his face —
'We'll be together, saved by grace.' "

Light fills the glory of the dawn,
    Eternal home!
Glorious sunrise — earth's shadows gone!
Worship and praise around the throne,
    Hallelujah's ring
Worthy, worthy, worthy is my King.

                        Lovingly,

                        Margaret

Doris put another log on the fire, and we were once
again Mama and her children. The paneled walls,
bookcases, rockers with cushions, and the soft, red
carpet contrasted the old cookstove and the red

linoleum of earlier days when Mama had been young and strong.

Joyce remembered her acrobatic performances on the black bear rug, which had been a part of the family since the Wisconsin horse and buggy days. While Mama sewed or ironed, little Joyce had tumbled to her heart's content. But most of all she remembered the songs and stories from the rocking chair, and the security of Mama's lap, her harbor in the storms of childhood. Perhaps that memory made her the homebuilder she is, digging roots and erecting memories for her three children. The joy of a home is godliness and the beauty of a home is order. She learned well from Mama's lap.

Doris remembered the struggles of college, home and church, years in which she grew strong, and like a rock she became immovable in her faith. Perhaps she has some of Bestemor Bertilda in her that gives her the daring for new adventure. Her four children come often to her hearth and draw warmth from her faith. Like the godly woman described in Proverbs 31, she is a wife whose husband safely trusts in her.

Jeanelle, the fragile child, the beloved "baby," Mama's joy and Papa's delight. She was the protected one, and yet she grew in spiritual strength, and, like the palm tree, learned to bend with the wind and stand tall in the sun. Her two children see her as a tree planted by the rivers of water whose leaf never withers.

The room was quiet as the fire cast a warm glow over us as we sat — remembering. Doris brought in coffee and Mama spoke lovingly of how Papa enjoyed his children as adults, and the latter years being greater than the former.

I reminisced about Grace, at the age of 13, typing Papa's sermons and seemingly endless excerpts from theological volumes. She was never allowed to erase, but had to retype the entire page if she made a mistake. Papa probably secretly took credit for Grace winning a typing contest, and eventually having very responsible executive secretarial positions. Her work took her to London, and she was the first of the children to visit Norway. Grace didn't become the President's secretary, as Papa was sure she would, but had the joy of assisting at the great World Congress of Evangelism in Lausanne, Switzerland, sponsored by the Billy Graham Evangelistic Association. Papa would have thought that even more important.

Tonight Mama was listening to our stories. She loved it! When Joyce told how Papa called the honeymoon suite early in the morning and asked Howard if his Solveig was all right, we all rocked with laughter.

Doris told of slipping into Papa's church, during an unplanned visit. When Papa saw her he announced, "We will have a solo from Mrs. Hammer after the offering." She protested that it was Joyce who was the soloist. "All my children sing!" he insisted, but Doris stood her ground. No, she didn't sing. "Vot do you do?" Doris shook her head "Nothing." "After the offering, you vill lead in prayer." Papa was not to be outdone.

During one communion service an elderly deacon refused to partake. "I can't take communion. I have been living in sin." He went on to explain, "I have been living with this woman who is at my side, and I can't remember marrying her."

Papa left the communion table and comforted the weeping deacon, "Take communion, brother. You aren't living in sin. I remember your wedding; I married you many years ago. We all forget sometimes." Papa's congregation smiled and nodded to each other. They were all growing old together; they understood.

Mama, always full of humor, couldn't resist telling about the elderly "tanta" who idolized her nephew, Villie. She went about the church giving everyone her happy report. "Villie is in the army and so smart. He got a promotion and I can't remember vot it vas, but it has a 'ral' on the end of it, like gen-ral."

One Sunday morning Tanta was late and arrived just as Papa announced the opening hymn. When Tanta walked through the door, the congregation stood to its feet. With head high and eyes shining, she walked to the front and faced the congregation, "Sit down, good people. Sit down. I vas vunce no better than you. I found out vot Villie's promotion vas." With a sigh of pride she announced. "My Villie is a corporal."

Papa offered his congratulations and again announced the opening hymn. Papa's church nodded and smiled.

The years had come and gone so fast and now the joy of laughter and relief from tears brought the "all years" together for good.

Grace wrapped our evening up by telling the story of the sweater.

"I remember hearing of the time Mama was very ill at the children's home, and was waiting for the ambulance to take her to the hospital. Four or five of the nursery children came into her room and she had to caution them, 'Please don't touch me. I'm very sick, please don't touch the bed. It hurts me.' So the little children sat quietly watching over her from the other twin bed across the room. A sweater of hers was on the bed. One child picked it up and held it tight. The little fellow next to him wanted to hold a piece of it too, and quickly the sweater was stretched across the long string of laps, with each child clutching a fistful of it. One way or another they would reach out to her."

I thought about us, Mama's children. We were like those young children. Each one of us held a part of Mama, and in holding we gave love back to her, and to each other.

Mama smiled and listened. She had made a promise to God and God had made a promise to her: All her children would be taught of the Lord. Her children were safe under the shadow of the Almighty.

It was time to say good night. Before Joyce took Mama across the road to sleep in her own bed, we held her close and sang the song Gordon and Alice had composed together, a favorite blessing song:

> The blessing of the Lord be upon you
> We bless you in the name of the Lord.

P.S. In a box in my hand I hold two treasures:
Papa's sermons, and Mama's gray sweater.
In my heart they blend as one:
Papa's theology and Mama's living —
God's grace and love.

twenty-one

The Dress

MAMA SAT ROCKING GENTLY, the bright wool afghan wound around her bony knees. Staring out across the quiet lake below our house, she sang softly to herself. A far-away look filled her eyes, her mind was somewhere in the "long ago." Janice, who had come for a visit, heard her murmur, "Love and forgive. Love and forgive."

"Bestemor, you are talking to yourself again," Jan laughed as she pulled up a stool to snuggle close to her. The house was quiet with the contentment that comes when those you love have returned home and are close by your side.

Pressing Mama's thin, blue-veined hand against her own soft, younger cheek, Jan asked, "What were you reading?"

Mama stroked the open Bible lovingly. "When you stand praying, forgive" (Mark 11:25).

"But, Bestemor, there are some things you can't forgive."

157

I knew Jan was in for a story.

Stroking Jan's soft blond hair, Bestemor rocked a little slower and added, "I'll tell you a story, Janice. We'll call the girl Mary and the man John.

"It happened a long time ago." I reached for my coffee cup and listened from the kitchen. I had heard the story a few days before, but had promised not to tell it.

Bestemor's white hair framed her gentle face, and her blue eyes held that far-away look. Jan waited. These were moments she would hold in her heart forever. She would remember, and tell her children.

"Mary was young, filled with dreams of love for her husband, John, and her love for God and His service. John, restless and impatient in his new pastorate in the farmlands of Wisconsin, longed for the libraries and action of New York City or Chicago, where he had attended seminary. John's brilliant mind craved books. Mary saw beauty in everything — the smell of the freshly plowed fields, the song of a bird, the first signs of spring, crocuses and violets.

"She tied her tiny daughter to her lap while she drove the horse and buggy to the country church. John would ride with Deacon Olsen to gather parishioners along the way. Mary sang to the wind and laughed with the birds. But she had one secret longing, a new dress for spring. Not the somber brown or black, befitting a minister's wife, but a soft voile billowing dress with lace around the neck and sleeves, and a big sash. There was no money! Carefully she laid plans: She would put pennies into a box until there was enough money to buy a new kerosene lamp for John and material for a new dress. She would reuse the lace from an old velvet dress in the trunk. Someday she would make a blue velvet dress for baby Louise.

"The day came when the treadle machine purred like music while Mary sang and sewed. Golden-haired Louise played with empty spools and clothes pins. The small house shone, clean. The new lamp had a place of honor on John's reading table. Violets filled a bowl on the starched tablecloth, and cups were placed for afternoon coffee when John would return home.

"In a playful mood, Mary pulled down her long brown hair, brushed it in the morning sun. Then she put on her new dress, soft pink voile with violets and lace. A sash tied in the back and Mary swung around to the delightful squeals of Louise. It was spring! She was young, just twenty-three, with another new life within her and Louise to rock and love. The wilderness church, the somber immigrants tilling the land, and the severe harshness of long winters had isolated the young wife into her world of poetry and song. She grew to love the faithful people and shared their joys and sorrows.

"But today was spring and she danced with abandoned joy in her new billowing dress.

"With the flash of summer lightning, Mary was whirled around by an angry John, whose storm of frustration unleashed the fury within him. 'Money for foolishness! No libraries, no books — no one to talk to about anything except cows and chickens, planting and harvest.' Like a smoldering volcano, John erupted with rage and ripped the dress to shreds. Just as suddenly the storm was over, and the galloping hoofs of John's horse broke the quiet terror. As he rode into the wind he unleashed the remainder of his fury on the passing fields and their wide-eyed cows and clucking chickens. He longed to gallop from Wisconsin to the heart of New York — his beloved library.

"Huddled in a corner, Mary clutched Louise and the shredded dress. Trembling with fear and anger she remained motionless. Too drained to weep, she was sick with an emptiness and an unutterable longing for her mother in New York. There was no one to turn to in that lonely farmland. She remembered Psalm 34:4: 'I sought the LORD, and He heard me, and delivered me from all my fears.' Then she wept, long and deep, and cried unto the Lord."

Bestemor paused. "Be slow to cry to man, Janice, but let your cry be unto God." She rocked slowly, then continued.

"Mary set her heart to seek a way of escape. She would make a pallet up in the loft and take Louise to sleep with her. John would sleep alone. Then she folded the shredded dress in a small package and hid it in her trunk. Pastor Hansen was coming to visit the rural churches and Mary decided to bide her time, to quietly wait and show the dress to Pastor Hansen, then ask for assistance to leave John and return to New York. With quiet determination she put on her dark dress and combed her long brown hair into a severe knot, befitting a minister's wife. She set the table for supper. When John returned late in the night his supper was in the warming oven. Mary was asleep in the loft with Louise curled in her arm.

"Quietly John ate his supper and looked for Mary. When he found her in the loft, he ordered her back to their bed and put Louise in her crib. Mary gently tucked Louise in her crib and obediently went to bed.

John's storm had passed, but he was unaware of the debris in its wake.

"Life went on as usual, but the song was gone and Mary's steps were weighted with bitterness. She quietly waited and thought out her plans.

"The arrival of Pastor Hansen brought a new exuberance to John as the two ministers discussed books and theology and the work of the church conference. Mary served quietly. No one would have guessed the anguish behind her gentle face as she worshipped with the faithful congregation, but heard little of the sermons.

"The final service was drawing to a close and, as yet, Mary had not had the opportunity to see Pastor Hansen alone. She had to find the opening, perhaps this Sunday afternoon, when John would visit a shut-in member while Pastor Hansen would meditate on the evening message. With a quickened mind she decided to listen to the sermon and perhaps use his comments as an opening.

"'The text this morning is found in Mark 11:25: "When ye stand praying, forgive." Forgiveness is not optional, but a command. Forgiveness is not a feeling, but an act of faith, a definite act of the will to forgive, in obedience to God's command. The feeling comes later, the feeling of peace. When we offer to God our hurts and despair, God will pour his love and compassion into the wounds and His healing will come.'

"'Oh, no,' Mary cried inside. 'I can't forgive, and I can never forget!'

"The sermon continued, 'Someone may be thinking "I can never forget, even if I could forgive." You are right, you can't forget, but you needn't be devastated by the remembering. God's love and His forgiveness can and will cushion the memory until the imprint is gone. When you forgive you must destroy the evidence, and remember only to love. "For God so loved the world, that He gave His only begotten Son, that whosoever believeth in Him should not perish, but have everlasting life." In closing let us stand and say the Lord's prayer. "Forgive us our debts, as we forgive our debtors." '

"John and Pastor Hansen rode home with Deacon Olsen. Mary stepped into her buggy, tied her wide black hat with a scarf, and carefully secured Louise around her waist. As the horse, Dolly, trotted briskly down the country road, Mary's scalding tears poured forth.

"She knew what she must do. She would obey God. Without waiting to unhitch Dolly, she fled from the buggy and placed sleeping Louise in her crib. With trembling hands she took out of the trunk the package with the torn dress, but she couldn't let go. The Sunday dinner was in the warming oven; Mary poked the fire and added more wood. Automatically she put on the coffee pot and set the table. 'The evidence must go' rang in her memory. 'I forgive you, John.' She finally picked up the tattered dress with one hand and the stove lid with the other. Tears splashed on the fire and the dress burned slowly.

"'True forgiveness destroys the evidence' pounded so loudly in her heart that she failed to hear John's footsteps. 'Mary, what are you doing?' Trembling with sobs, she said, 'I am destroying the evidence.'

"To herself she said, 'My offering to God.'

"Then John remembered! Pale and shaken he murmured, 'Please forgive me.' "

Bestemor rocked quietly.

"Please, Grandmother, what happened?" Jan begged. Bestemor waited. Her eyes followed the ducks on the lake, but her heart was somewhere else. Softly she continued:

"Now John has gone home. Fifty-eight years together, and I miss him."

Wide-eyed with understanding, Jan wrapped her arms around her beloved Bestemor! "That was you and Grandfather!" The chair rocked slowly in the quiet room as Bestemor's loving hand stroked the bowed head.

I slipped quietly down the path of fallen leaves to the lake to feed the ducks. The four white pet geese honked majestically across the lake as I drank deeply of the cool autumn breeze and felt the burden of old hurts slowly ebbing away. God's cushioning love heals old scars.

P.S. A few days later Mama had a dream. Three angels appeared to her and said, "Come, we are going to a celebration." Over the arm of one angel was draped a beautiful dress.

twenty-two

Golden Threads

MAMA LAID ASIDE HER KNITTING NEEDLES and closed the empty basket that had once been full of yarn. Out of bits and pieces of leftover yarn, Mama had woven a beautiful afghan of many colors. Spreading her handiwork over her lap she looked up with a smile, "This one goes to Heather." Mama wanted to remind her first great-grandchild that God wcrks all things together for good. We need the rain as well as the sunshine: we need the bits and pieces of life to make the whole. When woven together by God's hand of love, life is beautiful.

Nearly fifty years had passed since I had found Mama's diary, and tonight I remembered her wistful, "Someday I'll tell you the rest of the story."

Grace, the efficient secretary, had put the family history in writing through the letters she wrote on Mother's behalf to all of us. The door to the past was gently opening and the notes to Gordon had been the beginning:

Dictated by mother
to Grace
September 19, 1971

To Gordon Lund Tweten,

In the 1700s some of the Lunds left England. In the service of the king (Denmark and Norway had one king) they were enroute to Denmark but shipwrecked off the coast of Norway. Right there, outside of Lista, they settled.

Being very wealthy (it is said that they carried their wealth with them in barrels) they established and built the city of Farsund, including the city's first church.

The Lund family house estate was called Husan and today is the city hall of Farsund, my family having given the house and property to the city. A Norwegian landmark, the building is still called Husan.

King Oscar II planted four trees on the city hall grounds in memory of my grandfather Eilert and his three brothers. Although the trees have recently been replanted, a memorial plaque marks each tree.

In World War II the Germans accidentally set fire to Husan, not knowing that the fireplace wasn't open for use; but the building has been restored to its original appearance. On the mantel is a model of the ship my forebears traveled in from England.

After my grandfather died, my grandmother never remarried; she didn't want to lose the name "Lund," for it gave her direct access to the king in case she needed help.

At the age of fifteen, with money left by my grandmother, I came to the United States and later paid for my wedding. Because my mother married out of her class she was disinherited.

But in her notes to Gordon, Mama had not finished the story; now, five years later, Mama was ready to give me the missing pieces. Sitting by the fire, she looked out over the lake and watched the ducks and geese in formation. I waited, cup of coffee in hand. Slowly, thoughtfully, Mama spoke.

"When my mother was only sixteen she defied her parents, the powerful Lunds of Farsund, and married a dashing, handsome seaman, Ole Jorgen Johannessen. My grandparents carried out their threats and disinherited her. Joseph and I were born in Lista. Since my father was out to sea for long periods of time, his older brother was the guardian of the young family. My austere aunt and uncle had no children. They resented my young mother and declared her incompetent to care for us children, so they took us and the income entrusted to us away from my mother, and looked for ways to descredit her. Instead of reconciling with her own family and requesting their help, my mother stubbornly set her plans to flee to America.

"I remember the day she came to take us away from my uncle and aunt. I didn't understand what was happening, but they refused to let us go with her. We watched in silence as she walked down the road, away from us, sobbing. I cried, 'Mor, Mor' and tried to follow her, but my aunt pulled me back. They scolded, 'Don't call her Mor, call her Tilda.' I was only four and one half years old, but I can still remember how I lifted my head high and defiantly answered, 'Min Mor.' A visiting neighbor asked, 'Where does that child get such airs?' My aunt answered disdainfully, 'She is a Lund!'

"Joseph and I knew we were involved in a tragedy, but we were obedient children. We deeply resented our father who chose to believe distortions rather than defend our mother. I had also grown up believing that my grandmother Lund had forsaken my mother. During my teens I went to school, and worked in a plant nursery. My heart was a record of my hurts.

"When I was 15, I received an inheritance from Grandmother Lund, who had died earlier. Joseph, my brother, had already come to America. Now it was time for me to sail, to join my mother and Joseph who was 16 years old."

We sat quietly by the fire. I was remembering my grandmother, Bertilda, proud and independent. Because I had been born on her birthday she always sent me a special birthday card with a one-dollar bill in it. At Christmas time we received handknit long woolen stockings, a welcome gift for the cold Canadian winters. When I was six years old, Mama gave me a small umbrella. That was my most prized possession. But not until I was older did I understand that it was because her mother had sent her an umbrella when she was six years old that she gave me one, too. As a young child Mama had said, "When I have a little girl I will buy her an umbrella." When our own Janice was six years old, Mama bought her a small umbrella and told her how she had treasured her own as a child.

I thought of the grace of God: permitting Uncle Joe and Mama to live in Brooklyn near Bestemor during her last years. Now I realized Mama's cry which Jeanelle heard was the sob of a child for her lost mother, rather than Mama's cry over present grief. But what about Mama's father?

To my question Mama answered slowly, "Years later he found out the truth, but it was too late. He even came to America, but the barrier of pride was greater than the ocean. When he returned to Norway, I was told that he spent hours walking by the sea, grieving over the loss of his wife and children. One night he walked late into the cold wind, the ocean spraying his clothes. He died of pneumonia, but friends said he really died from a broken heart.

"When I came to America, I also came to know the love of God. I gave my life to Jesus Christ. As a new Christian, the first thing I did was make a list of my resentments and any unforgiveness. I wrote down the names of the people who hurt me, I forgave them, and then I began to pray for them. My father was first on the list, then my aunt and uncle. Everyone on my list has become a Christian, but first I had to love and forgive. When my father came to America I told him of my love and forgiveness. I also had an opportunity to talk with my aunt and uncle. They, too, learned God's love and forgiveness. I'm told that my father died in peace, knowing Jesus. The day will come when God will wipe all tears away."

I thought about God's ways, and His order for life. I thought about rebellion and pride, and the years of heartache that so often follow. If we allowed God's love and forgiveness to flow freely, the heartaches of life could be so simply washed away. Simple, but not easy. God's way, not man's way.

Mama had walked a road of simple obedience to God's ways. In her daily discipline of walk she had found His yoke easy and His burden light. And she had gently opened squeaking doors to the past and oiled them with joy so her children could walk through those doors, not remembering hurts, but only the all-encompassing love of God.

The days moved rapidly into the Christmas season, and with it came the activity of holiday preparation. Our daughter, Janice, flew in from Massachusetts early so she could spend more time with Bestemor — "Just in case it should be her last

Christmas." Jan spent many happy hours asking questions and making notes of her grandmother's wisdom. Ralph, our youngest son, taped her readings and songs. For every occasion Mama had a story. I kept them in my heart.

One morning Mama stopped us in our busy holiday preparation and asked us to sit down. In her lap was the morning mail. With trembling hands she held a letter from Norway that contained two small silk treasures, each the size of a postcard.

"This is like a gift from God, Janice," she added softly. "I was never sure that my grandmother Lund had forgiven my mother for her rebellion. Now it seems that an angel brought me this special message." We sat quietly. As she read the beautifully embroidered words on the delicate silk, Mama was deeply moved. She read in Norwegian first then translated for us. "Congratulations on your birthday, my little Rose, my dearly beloved Tilda. God give you many happy returns of the day." The other read, "Live well, my Tilda, God is love. Take the cross and follow Him from life until death."

"Janice, these words were embroidered by your great, great grandmother Lund on April 18, 1874. On this earth I will never know why the message never reached my mother, but someday I shall know. To think that one hundred years later I receive the answer to one of my heart's questions, the unspoken words of love and forgiveness etched with tiny threads. These treasures were found and mailed to me by an elderly relative. She had no idea what this message would mean to me, but God did!"

The golden thread of love that binds us all together will continue to join one generation to the next. "LORD, Thou hast been our dwelling place in all generations."

"I wish my brother Joe could have read this," Mama added wistfully.

I remembered my uncle Joe as a big, lovable, prosperous businessman in New York. Today Mama was remembering him as her five-and-a-half-year-old brother, who held her hand as they watched their mother leave for America. When Joe was 15, he left for America, growing into manhood in the new land. Like Mama, his faith in God grew deeper every year. When he was older death took his wife, Hilda, and his beautiful daughter, Esther, but his faith never wavered. Later, like a burst of sunshine, Tanta Agatha walked into Uncle Joe's lonely life, and the two of them have blessed us all. God has taken Uncle Joe home, but Tanta Agatha remains our beloved link to the past generation.

I was brought back to the present. "To everything there is a season," Mama was saying. "There is a time to remember and a time to forget. Always there is the time to love and forgive."

Mama held the silk tapestry in her hand and softly added, "These are golden threads to complete my memory of Husan — beloved Husan and the Lunds.

"They are home now, Janice, and soon I will join them — in God's Husan.

"Now it is Christmas, a time to rejoice. Just as this message of love came to me from out of the past, so God's message of love has come to us for almost two thousand years. 'For God so loved the world, that

He gave His only begotten Son, that whosoever believeth in Him should not perish, but have everlasting life' (John 3:16).

"It is time for Christmas, but first we have coffee."

twenty-three

The Envelope

"DON'T FORGET THE ENVELOPE, DEAR." Grace eased Mama's frail form against the soft pillows, and covered her cold hands with the lacy wool stole Joyce had sent from Chicago.

"No, Mama, I won't forget."

The snow swirled around the house, piling drifts along the street, which brought traffic to a halt. It was Sunday, January 9, 1977, when Greensboro, North Carolina was engulfed in a record-breaking blizzard.

Jeanelle, notified of Mama's weakening heart condition, was flying from sunny Florida. Joyce, with her son Steve who was returning to the University of North Carolina, was coming for a planned visit. Doris had arrived earlier, before the storm. Grace, who lived nearby, made it safely to our home before the streets became impassable. Tonight Mama's children would try to be together. Since the airport was closed, power lines down, and phone service disrupted, we could only wait and pray.

Harold, my husband, kept the logs blazing in the fireplace and wood piled high on the porch. The power lines held and the house was warm. Doris kept the coffee pot hot.

Grace continued to rock quietly and hum old familiar hymns while the oxygen bubbled softly to ease Mama's difficult breathing. How thankful I was to be a nurse and able to care for her in our home. How good God is to all of us to allow us to be a part of the sharing of the "sweater," each of us holding a piece of her care. Jeanelle and her husband had held a part in Florida when Papa went "home." Doris and David had built the dream house in Stoneville. Grace managed the details of practical business affairs.

With a warm fire and a cup of tea, Harold had opened his arms to our gentle Mama. Howard had sent Joyce on her mission of love to each home. She had quietly helped out wherever needed. Whether weddings or funerals, Joyce had been there, a present help in time of need. Now we would all be together.

Christmas had been a joyous time with family and friends. Messages from grandchildren winged their love across the miles from Germany, Oklahoma, New York, Massachusetts, Arkansas, Chicago, Virginia, and Florida. The highlight was a Christmas luncheon we had for the senior citizens of the First Baptist Church of Stoneville. The Reverend Mr. Ward Burch led the delegation and Mama rejoiced with her church family by giving her Christmas reading and sharing stories from Canada. The final carol, "Silent Night," echoed long after Mama waved to the last car turning the road and crossing over the bridge on the lake. Mama knew in her heart there soon would be another crossing for her and many of her friends. "Lead me gently home, Father," she added softly.

"Just finished my rounds at Wesley Long Hospital and decided to check on Mama before going home." Mama patted Dr. Bruce with a "Thank you, dear," while he listened to her heart.

"She is about the same, but keep her comfortable, and don't forget, this jeep gets through anything." Then he was gone into the swirling snow.

My thoughts went back to Christmas again and I could hear Mama in times past, "No one celebrates Christmas like a Norwegian." Mama had sent two hundred Christmas cards, with a picture of her and her open Bible, to friends and family in Norway, Canada, and America. Each envelope contained a personal note.

Gifts had been planned for everyone in the family: afghans, shawls, quilts, or a piece of china. Birthday cards, each with two dollars enclosed, had been put aside for birthdays ahead. Thank you notes had been written. Each drawer was neatly arranged. Her desk was in order and her knitting basket closed. The open Bible, with a marker, lay by her bedside. She knew where the next reading would begin. During the past year Mama had read her Bible through four times. When I read out loud to her, she was aware of any skipped verses or words, even the "begats."

In her Bible she kept a letter which I had written to her a long time ago, and yet, it seems like yesterday:

For her birthday, March 3, 1952

Darling Mother,

Can it be another birthday? And with that special

day there comes the long, long trail awinding into the land of memories.

It seems only yesterday that hushed, excited voices whispered in corners about that present for you. The long, happy hours of roaming through dime-store counters, with only a few pennies to spend, can't be so many years back.

Remember the smudgy cards with all our names in childish scrawl? We promised you pink silk dresses and satin shoes. No wonder you smiled. You knew that life is made of cotton and leather, and that dreams don't always come true.

Perhaps your eyes will never see a home of luxury, but across the miles you see your children standing in their places, strong in body and serving your God. Your ears may never wear diamonds, but always you'll hear words of love and devotion. The ermine wraps may fall across other shoulders, but you'll always know the strength of young arms when your shoulders stoop. The pink silk dress will some day be the robe of righteousness in all its beauty. Could diamond rings make a mother's hand more beautiful? That hand so steady to guide, so tender to love and strong when other hands were weak. Somehow, the memory of those hands folded in prayer bring renewed courage for the days ahead. But what about those tired feet in satin slippers? The miles are endless, the walks to church and visiting the sick, the round of shopping with only pennies to count, the tread of sorrow and nights of sickness. Still the feet go on, in countless ways of walking through valleys of disappointment and up the hills of hope and climbing the mountains victorious. And when those feet get too tired, there will be six rocking chairs and satin slippers by the fireside of six thankful children.

So, today is mother's birthday, and what can we send? With God's help we'll send six Christian children, loving and serving the same Jesus mother loves and serves.

Your Margaret

The storm continued with unabated fury and sent pines crashing into the woods, breaking the eerie silence with loud cannon-like booms. We kept our watch, and waited. The hours seemed endless. Suddenly the phone shattered the silence, and Grace shouted, "They are safe in Raleigh, and special transportation has been arranged." Four hours later we heard the sound of a vehicle and saw the welcome headlights coming over the bridge of the lake.

Jeanelle, in Florida clothes, was shivering and Steve was bursting with the story of Jeanelle and Joyce's surprise meeting in the airport.

"Believe me, Aunt Margaret, the entire airport could hear them running to each other, shouting, 'How did you get here?'" It was 10 P.M. They had been enroute for 12 hours. But now they were safe and warm. Doris had supper waiting.

Mama looked up to see her five daughters. With a "Praise the Lord," she dozed off to sleep, while the fury of the storm increased.

The upstairs of my home looked like a college dormitory with quilts, blankets, and open suitcases covering the entire floor. We somehow knew this was a special time and sensed that cord of love drawing us close. We agreed to take turns in watching over Mama. I took the night watch.

The house was quiet, broken only by the sounds of logs crackling in the fireplace. Harold continued to pile up wood in case the power went off.

I held Mama tenderly and prayed for her, then tucked her in like a fragile child. The medication and oxygen eased her discomfort and she was soon asleep. I sat in her chair and rocked. Night duty was no stranger to me.

I had spent countless hours at the bedside of critically ill patients and I realized how few of them made preparation for their journey home. But I thought of the envelopes that had winged across the miles carrying messages in familiar script, adding a dimension of faith for Mama's children. I thought also about the envelopes she had mailed to each of her grandchildren:

December 1969

Dear Dan,

Grandpa and I thought that this Christmas season would be a perfect time to give all sixteen grandchildren, as well as Heather Dawne, the first great-grandchild on her first Christmas, the little inheritance we have planned on for some time. The enclosed bond is not much, but with it we want you to know that we love you and wish the best in life for you. The very best, always, is to know the Lord Jesus as your own personal Savior and to live for Him.

Put the bond away in a safe place — at least until its maturity date — and then use it for something special. When I was four years old my grandmother died, and she had put away some money for me which I used for my wedding when I was twenty one. Proverbs 13:22 says: "A good man leaveth an inheritance to his children's children." Keep this letter with your bond. May God bless you always.

Lovingly, your grandma,

Ella Tweten

Then there was the evening, not so long ago, when she asked us five sisters to sit down. We knew she had something special to say when she handed each one of us another envelope. "It is good to leave an inheritance to your children," she said. Each envelope contained five hundred dollars. "It is good to follow God's order."

Although Gordon was gone, Mama included Alice, his wife, in the inheritance. Mama shared the response from Alice.

Brooklyn, New York
November 1976

My mom,

Your letter, with the check, was read and became a benediction on our Thanksgiving gathering. A picture at that time of the faces and reaction was beautiful to see. What the Lord said to me was, "Do you see, Alice, love is eternal. You have known human love. Human love is fleeting. My love is eternal through My Son."

So thank you, Mor, for the love of Jesus flowing through you. It touched the hearts of our family. Only God knows what your love gift meant to them.

Jeg Elsker Dey (I love you),

Alice

I opened Mama's Bible and read:

But continue thou in the things which thou hast learned and hast been assured of, knowing of whom thou hast learned them; And that from a child thou hast known the holy scriptures, which are able to make thee wise unto salvation through faith which is in Christ Jesus (2 Tim. 3:14-15). For I am now ready

to be offered, and the time of my departure is at hand.
I have fought a good fight, I have finished my course,
I have kept the faith (2 Tim. 4:6-7).

I closed the Bible and opened yet another envelope
I had found.

Mother's prayers for her children,
November 1975 (By Jeanelle)

Mother and I were enjoying a quiet morning
together in her home. We had had an early breakfast
and then moved on into the living room where she
settled in her rocking chair and I settled comfortably
on the floor near her. We talked of many things,
especially that she would perhaps be going "home"
soon. We discussed the Old Testament patriarchs
who seemed to know when it was time to leave their
earthly dwelling. They made preparation for their
families by praying for each other and bestowing a
special "blessing" upon each one. As we talked
together, I believe God was motivating us to think
in the same direction because when I said, "Mother,
wouldn't it be something if God would give you a
special prayer or a special blessing for each of your
five daughters?"

She immediately responded with, "Wouldn't that
be wonderful. Yes, yes, I somehow believe He may
want to do that."

Like the patriarchs of old, Mama also bestowed her
own special prayer of blessing on each daughter.
Mama, in her orderly way, had not only placed an
earthly inheritance in our hands; but in our hearts
she placed her blessing of faith.

Long before the dawn came quietly over the frozen
lake and cast streaks of light over the snow banks,
Grace slipped downstairs to take my place. I slept

soundly until the dormitory upstairs came to life and I could smell the coffee and bacon in the kitchen. Joyce was serving Mama's Norwegian pancakes. That was motivation enough for action. The storm shut us in from the outside world.

After a restful night Mama was strong enough to be propped up in bed while we brought our coffee cups to sit beside her. We took turns reading the Bible and singing her favorite songs, some in halting Norwegian. We thanked her for the gift of love to us and once again the stories came with tears and laughter. At one time she looked up at us, "My escort to heaven." Another time she said, "I love him," and we quickly added, "Oh, we know you love the Lord, Mama." With a twinkle in her eye she said, "I was talking about Papa."

There were joyous hours around the piano, quiet times of reading to Mama. We bathed and dressed her in her soft pink gowns and propped her up with pillows. She automatically folded her hands in a blessing when we held a cup to her lips. There was a rest for her in the love from her children.

By Thursday the streets were clear enough for Pastor Wilson Stewart to visit and hold a Communion service. In conclusion we sang: "Surely goodness and mercy shall follow me, all the days, all the days of my life."

During the night watch, when Harold was sitting with her, Mama called out, "Mor, Mor," with the cry of a child. At other times she talked to the children at the children's home. Friday morning she was weaker, but aware of her children kneeling by the bed expressing our love to God and to her for our beautiful mother. There was a hush in the winter wonderland where the snow was piled in drifts over fences and bushes.

Toward evening our youngest son, Ralph, slipped in quietly with a gentle kiss and saying as he stroked her forehead, "This is Ralph, I love you, Grandma." She murmured softly, "Ya, ya, praise the Lord."

We sang an old song from the church string band days, "I will meet you in the morning, Just inside the Eastern Gate." And then another song in the Norwegian language, "He the Pearly Gates Will Open."

A quiet peace settled over the house, and we were wrapped in the amber glow of love. Softly, gently she entered into His presence. We felt the touch of the Master's hand as we rose to our feet. With hearts and hands united, we sang: "Praise God, from whom all blessings flow."

Mama had gone home to meet her King.

Sunday morning the church bells rang out across the frozen snow. Huddled in woolen scarves and coats the worshipers braced themselves against the icy winds to attend the worship service at First Baptist Church, in Stoneville.

Joyce and Grace sat quietly in Mama's pew, while Pastor Ward Burch made the announcement.

"Our beloved friend, Elvine Tweten, went home to be with the Lord, Friday, January 14, at 7:45 P.M. The memorial service will be held here, at the church, at 2 P.M. today. We offer the family our love and prayers at this time."

When the ushers moved down the aisle to receive

the Sunday morning offering, Joyce remembered Mama's clear instructions to Grace, "Don't forget the envelope, dear."

With quiet reverence Joyce placed Mama's church offering in the plate. Her offering to God — a life of faith. Her offering on earth — the work of her hands.

"Verily I say unto you she did cast in all that she had, even *all her living*" (Mark 12:43-44).

Going Home

Walk a little slower, Child,
The pathway shorter seems.
I long to smell the flowers wild
Beside the flowing stream.

Sing a little louder, Bird,
As squirrels chase in play.
In the dawn your song is heard
As night shadows steal away.

Stay a little longer, Sun,
For nights are often long.
For me the sunset-time has come
And I must journey home.

Bloom a little longer, Rose,
As breezes kiss your cheek.
Too soon the strength of youth goes,
My trembling hands grow weak.

Stop a moment, Beloved One,
I need your strong firm arm
To hold me close within your love,
Sheltered from fear's alarm.

Sit awhile, Lovely Girl,
I'll tell you how time has flown,
For I, too, raced in life's mad whirl,
Tell me — where have years gone?

Slow your pace, Tall Lean Youth,
Bend your ear to hear,
For age speaks forth wisdom's truth,
Perfect love dispels all fear.

Stop your play, Little One,
Stand beside my rocking chair,
Together we'll watch the setting sun
And say our evening prayer.

Wait a little longer, Dear,
See the sun set o'er that hill,
Let me feel your warm hand near.
The evening breeze grows chill.

Wait a moment, Silver Cloud,
Don't pass before the sun,
My steps are slow, my head is bowed,
My race is almost run.

Turn a little slower, Earth,
From space I watch you pass,
Fjords — mountains — place of birth,
Oceans, rolling fields of grass.

Come a little closer, Lord,
Let me feel Your hand.
I staked my soul upon Your Word,
On Your promises I stand.

Hasten now the perfect dawn,
Good-by to shadows gray,
I leave you not to grieve or mourn.
Come quickly, Glorious Day.

I leave earth with a gentle sigh,
A caress for those I love,
As my spirit soars beyond the sky
With Him — Oh, perfect love.

The lights of home, the open gate,
The song of angel band,

Beloved faces there await,
And the touch of the Master's hand.

> Margaret T. Jensen
> January 21, 1977